SPECTRUM MATHS

▼

NUMBER

▲

Teacher's

2

Dave Kirkby

Collins Educational

Author
Dave Kirkby

Series and cover design
Sylvia Tate

Design
Perry Tate Design

Cover artwork
Katty McMurray

Artwork
Chantal Kees, Roy Mitchell, Lisa Williams

Published by Collins Educational
An imprint of HarperCollins*Publishers* Ltd
77–85 Fulham Palace Road
Hammersmith
London W6 8JB

First published 1999

ISBN 0 00 312746 X

British Library Cataloguing in Publication Data
A catalogue record for this book is available from the British Library.

Printed in Great Britain by Martins the Printers, Berwick-upon-Tweed

Contents

Introduction

The National Numeracy Strategy

The National Numeracy Project developed the Framework for Teaching Mathematics in the drive to improve standards in numeracy. The Framework comprises a set of yearly teaching programmes for National Curriculum mathematics, providing primary teachers with guidance for teaching the programmes of study at Key Stages 1 and 2. Specific yearly objectives are grouped into four strands, three for number – 'Knowledge of numbers and the number system', 'Calculations', 'Making sense of problems' – and a fourth for 'Shape and space'. Key objectives for each of the strands are highlighted and supplementary examples show what pupils should know, understand and be able to do by the end of the year.

The Framework's approach is based on daily mathematics lessons, focusing on **direct teaching** of the whole class and groups, and on mental calculation. The structure of the daily maths lesson reflects these principles:

▲ whole-class introduction, with an emphasis on oral
  work and mental calculation   (5–10 minutes)
▲ main teaching activity, which includes teaching input
  and pupil activities with the whole class, groups, pairs
  or individuals   (30–40 minutes)
▲ plenary session to conclude: work with the whole
  class to identify misconceptions and progress, summarise
  key facts, discuss next steps and set homework   (10–15 minutes)

Mathematics 5–14

In Scotland, the National Guidelines on Mathematics 5–14 provide the rationale and structure for the teaching of mathematics. The Guidelines offer five two-yearly levels of attainment A to E. The levels are divided into four attainment outcomes – 'Problem-solving and enquiry'; 'Information handling'; 'Number, money and measurement'; 'Shape, position and movement' – which give primary teachers a structure for organising appropriate programmes of study. Each outcome is subdivided into strands and targets which offer more detailed advice on the learning objectives. For many of the targets, examples are included to illustrate the depth of study and to suggest possible contexts for learning.

There has been an increasing focus on the importance of number, and on the effective development of strategies for mental calculation in particular. *Spectrum Maths – Number* can help teachers to improve their pupils' number skills by:

▲ offering clear learning objectives which can be referenced to the Guidelines;
▲ providing notes and activities to support direct, interactive teaching;
▲ indicating a structure for lessons;
▲ encouraging investigative learning and suggesting developments and extensions;
▲ highlighting key strategies for the effective development of mental skills;
▲ emphasising the use of simple practical equipment, games and puzzles.

Spectrum Maths – Number: an overview

Following the enormous success of the original series, *Spectrum Maths – Number* has been completely revised to fulfill the number requirements of the Framework for Teaching Mathematics and Maths 5–14. This number resource for Years 1–6 (P2–P7) provides teacher-led activities for the daily maths lesson.

Teacher's Books

There are six Teacher's Books in the series – one per year – offering a broad spectrum of number activities for the daily maths lesson. Each lesson features:

▲ clear number objectives, referenced to the Framework;
▲ suggestions for whole-class introductions and relevant mental strategies;
▲ key mathematical vocabulary;
▲ notes for the main lesson, a photocopiable activity or game to support group/pair work, and answers for quick reference;
▲ developments – ideas for adapting the activity for differentiation and extension;
▲ a list of materials needed;
▲ reference to the related individual activity in the Workbook or Pupil Book.

Every Teacher's Book also includes generic photocopy masters at the back, plus answers to all activities from the relevant Workbooks or Pupil Book.

Workbooks and Pupil Books

Two Workbooks for each of Years 1–2 (P2–P3) and one Pupil Book for each of Years 3–6 (P4–P7) provide individual practice linked to the main teaching activities. Each lesson in the Teacher's Book is cross-referenced to at least one page in the Workbook or Pupil Book and shares the same activity number. The pupil materials reinforce the main activities and are ideal for homework.

Planning and teaching with Spectrum Maths – Number

Spectrum Maths – Number is a flexible resource; it can be used alongside any main maths scheme to provide comprehensive number coverage. A correlation chart in each Teacher's Book (see pp. 8–9) provides an at-a-glance reference to *Spectrum* activities that meet the Framework's number objectives for that year.

All the activities have been written to aid interactive, direct teaching of the whole class, groups and pairs. The series also promotes other key teaching points from the Framework, including:

▲ ensuring that number facts and mental calculation methods are thoroughly established;
▲ emphasising the correct mathematical vocabulary and notation;
▲ extending lessons through activities that take place outside the maths lesson or at home.

Using Spectrum Maths – Number

Teacher's notes

▲ objectives and key vocabulary from the Framework

▲ whole-class introductions focusing on oral work (often includes mental strategies)

▲ notes for the main teaching activity (with answers where relevant)

▲ development ideas for differentiation and extension

▲ materials needed for the main activity and developments

▲3 Activity

Find the T

Key vocabulary

grid
pattern
row/column
square

Objectives

Counting and properties of numbers
▲ Count on or back in ones from any number
▲ Begin to count on in steps of 3, 4 or 5

Place value and ordering
▲ Read and write numbers to at least 100

Reasoning about numbers
▲ Recognise simple number patterns and predict

Introducing the activity

▲ Using squared paper, illustrate different ways of writing the numbers, in sequence, on a grid: along the rows, down the columns, left to right, right to left, top to bottom, bottom to top.
▲ Prepare different complete number grids. Hide individual numbers and sets of numbers (e.g. by covering them with cards, using Blu-tak). Ask the children to predict the hidden numbers. Remove the cards to check.

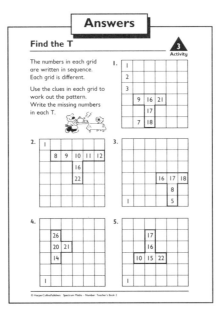

Main activity

▲ The children should test their predicted patterns on the grids, by counting, several times, before attempting to record the numbers in the T. Some children may want to write in the numbers outside the T.

Developments

▲ Children draw their own 6×6 grid, then draw a T shape, or some other shape. They decide on a rule for sequencing the numbers, and include one or two clues. After recording their own answer sheet, they could ask others to complete their grids.
▲ Extend to different sized grids, e.g. 8×8, or try rectangular grids.
▲ Create sequences which count in twos.
▲ Experiment with grids that use numbers following a spiral sequence.

Materials

▲ Squared paper
▲ Card
▲ Blu-tak

> **Individual practice in Workbook 2a**
> Activity 3: Missing numbers

▲3

14

▲ cross-reference to the related Workbook activity

Each activity in the Teacher's Book comprises a page of teacher's notes and a photocopiable pupil page for group/pair work. The Workbook activities provide individual practice linked to the lessons in the Teacher's Book and offer an ideal resource for homework.

Find the T

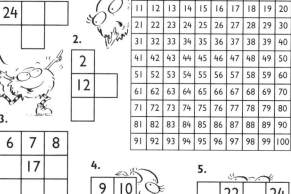

3
Activity

The numbers in each grid are written in sequence. Each grid is different.

Use the clues in each grid to work out the pattern. Write the missing numbers in each T.

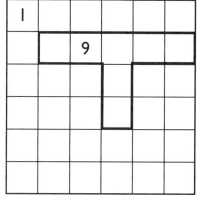

1.

1					
2					
3					
	9				
	7				

Pupil page

▲ photocopiable game or activity to support group/pair work

2.

1					
	9				

3.

1					

Workbook 2a

4.

	21				
1					

5.

1				

Missing numbers

3
Activity

Write the missing numbers in the squares.

1.

24		

1	2	3	4	5	6	7	8	9	10
11	12	13	14	15	16	17	18	19	20
21	22	23	24	25	26	27	28	29	30
31	32	33	34	35	36	37	38	39	40
41	42	43	44	45	46	47	48	49	50
51	52	53	54	55	56	57	58	59	60
61	62	63	64	65	66	67	68	69	70
71	72	73	74	75	76	77	78	79	80
81	82	83	84	85	86	87	88	89	90
91	92	93	94	95	96	97	98	99	100

2.

2	
12	

3.

6	7	8
	17	

4.

9	10	
	30	

5.

	22		24
		33	

6.

36	

7.

42	
62	

8.

15	
33	

9.

	89

5

Individual practice/homework

▲ at least one page linked to the Teacher's Book activity of the same number

▲ answers are included in the Teacher's Book

Correlation to the Framework

Spectrum activities for Year 2 number objectives

Key objectives are bold.

Summary of number objectives: Year 2		Activities in Teacher's Book 2
NUMBERS AND THE NUMBER SYSTEM		
Counting and properties of numbers	**Say the number names in order to at least 100, from and back to zero**	Opportunities in the introduction to most activities
	Count up to 100 objects by grouping them	
	Count on or back in ones or tens, from any two-digit number	3
	Count on in twos from and back to zero or any small number; **recognise odd and even numbers to at least 30**	22, 23, 36
	Count on in steps of 3, 4 or 5 to at least 30	3, 23, 35
	Begin to recognise multiples of 2, 5 or 10	18, 23, 35
Place value and ordering	**Read and write numbers to at least 100** in figures and words	3, 14, 16, 24, 29
	Know what each digit in a two-digit number represents, and partition two-digit numbers into tens and ones (TU)	5, 14, 16, 18, 22, 27, 29
	Say what is 1 or 10 more or less than any two-digit number	24
	Understand, use and begin to read the vocabulary of comparing and ordering numbers, including ordinal numbers to 100	5, 6, 14, 16, 18, 22, 27, 29, 40
	Compare two two-digit numbers, say which is more or less	5, 14, 16, 22, 27, 29, 40
	Order a set of one- and two-digit numbers, and position them on a number line	6, 14, 16
Estimating and rounding	Understand, use and begin to read the vocabulary of estimation	21, 38
	Round numbers less than 100 to the nearest 10	16, 29, 40
Fractions	Begin to recognise and find one half and one quarter of shapes and small numbers of objects; begin to know that two halves or four quarters make one whole and that two quarters = one half	19
CALCULATIONS		
Understanding addition and subtraction	Extend understanding of addition/subtraction and **recognise that addition can be done in any order**	1, 2, 4, 7, 9, 10, 12, 13, 15, 20, 21, 25, 26, 28, 29, 30, 31, 33, 37, 40
	Extend understanding that more than two numbers can be added, begin to add three single-digit numbers mentally (totals to 20) or three two-digit numbers with the help of apparatus	4, 10, 12, 26, 30, 31
	Begin to recognise that subtraction is the inverse of addition (subtraction reverses addition)	9, 15
Rapid recall of addition and subtraction facts	**Know by heart: addition and subtraction facts for all numbers to at least 10** all pairs of numbers with a total of 20 (eg 13 + 7, 6 + 14) all pairs of multiples of 10 with a total of 100 (eg 30 + 70)	1, 2, 4, 7, 9, 10, 13, 15, 20, 25, 26, 28, 30, 31, 32, 33, 37 20
Mental calculation strategies (+ and −)	**Use knowledge that addition can be done in any order to do mental calculations more efficiently:** for example, put the larger number first to count on or back in tens or ones add three small numbers by putting the largest number first and/ or find a pair totalling 10 partition into 5 and a bit when adding 6, 7, 8 or 9, then recombine (eg 16 + 8 = 15 + 1 + 5 + 3 = 20 + 4 = 24) partition additions into tens and units, then recombine	1, 9, 33 10, 12, 26, 30
	Find a small difference by counting up from the smaller to the larger number (eg 42 − 39)	2, 9, 13, 25, 29, 37, 40
	Identify near doubles, using doubles already known (eg 40 + 41)	
	Add/subtract 9/19 or 11/21: add/subtract 10/20 and adjust by 1	26

	Summary of number objectives: Year 2	Activities in Teacher's Book 2
Mental calculation *continued*	Use patterns of similar calculations	7, 30
	Use the corresponding addition/subtraction fact	15
	Use number facts and place value to add/subtract mentally	12, 31
	Bridge through 10 or 20, then adjust	20
Understanding multiplication and division	**Understand multiplication as repeated addition**, division as repeated subtraction or sharing; use the related vocabulary	17, 23, 39
	Recognise that multiplication can be done in any order	
	Recognise halving as the inverse of doubling	17
Rapid recall of multiplication and division facts	**Know: multiplication facts for the 2 and 10 times-tables doubles of all numbers to 10 and the corresponding halves** Begin to know: multiplication facts for the 5 times-table Derive quickly: division facts for the 2 and 10 times-tables doubles of all numbers to at least 15 (eg 11 + 11 or 11 × 2) doubles of multiples of 5 to at least 50 (eg 20 × 2 or 35 × 2) halves of multiples of 10 to 100 (eg half of 70)	39 17 39 39 17
Mental (× and ÷) strategies	Use known number facts and place value to multiply or divide by 2, 5 or 10	
Checking results	Repeat addition or multiplication in a different order	
	Check with an equivalent calculation	

MAKING SENSE OF PROBLEMS

Making decisions	**Choose and use appropriate** operation(s) and **ways of calculating to solve numerical problems**	Opportunities in many main activities or 'developments'
Reasoning about numbers or shapes	Solve mathematical problems or puzzles, recognise simple patterns and relationships, generalise and predict. Suggest extensions by asking 'What if...?' or 'What could I try next'?	1, 3, 4, 5, 7, 10, 12, 13, 14, 16, 18, 20, 25, 26, 27, 28, 30, 32, 35, 36
	Investigate a general statement about familiar numbers/shapes	13, 14, 16, 26, 27
	Explain methods and reasoning orally or in writing	2, 5, 10, 18, 26, 27, 37
Problems involving 'real life' or money	Solve simple word problems involving numbers in 'real life' or money, including finding totals, giving change, and working out which coins to pay; explain how the problem was solved	12, 31
	Recognise all coins and begin to use £.p notation for money	12, 31
Problems involving measures	Use and begin to read the vocabulary related to measures; **measure and compare:** using suitable non-standard units (eg paces, marbles, mugs); **using standard units (m, cm, kg, litre);** **suggest suitable units and measuring equipment** to estimate or **measure length, mass or capacity;** **use a ruler to measure lines that are a multiple of 1 cm**, and a metre stick to measure lines that are a multiple of 10 cm; **read a simple scale** to the nearest labelled division, recording estimates and measurements as 'about 8 centimetres' etc.	6, 21, 38 38 6, 21 21, 38 21, 38 21
	Use the vocabulary of time; use and know the relationships between units (second, minute, hour, day, week, month, year); suggest suitable units to estimate or measure time; order the months of the year; read the time to the hour, half-hour or quarter hour on an analogue or digital clock, and understand the notation 7:30	8 8
	Solve simple word problems involving measures or time	
Data handling	Collect, represent, **extract and interpret numerical data presented in simple charts and tables**: eg Venn or Carroll diagrams (two criteria), simple block graphs and tables	6, 11, 21, 24, 34, 38

Note: This chart is based on the August 1998 draft of the Framework for Teaching Mathematics, the most recent draft available at the time of printing. Teachers are advised to check these objectives against the final, published Framework.

Activity 1

Card adding

Key vocabulary

add
addition
pair
most/least
subtraction

Objectives

Understanding addition and subtraction
▲ Understand the operations of addition and subtraction and recognise that addition can be done in any order

Rapid recall of addition and subtraction facts
▲ Know addition and subtraction facts for numbers to 10

Mental calculation strategies (addition)
▲ Count on in ones

Reasoning about numbers
▲ Solve mathematical problems and recognise simple number patterns

Introducing the activity

▲ Demonstrate how the children can use an outline of the addition as a template on which to place the number cards each time.

$$\Box + \Box = \Box$$

▲ Form an addition using the template and the cards, e.g. 5 + 3. Rehearse addition, using a number line (1–10) to illustrate counting on to the correct answer.

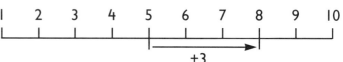

▲ Rehearse commutativity, i.e. 3 + 5 = 5 + 3, again using the number line to show that the answer is the same.

Main activity

▲ Encourage the children to work systematically, e.g. start by making all the additions possible with 1 as the first card.
▲ Discuss pairs, e.g. 5 + 2 and 2 + 5. Suggest that for this activity they are the same addition.

Developments

▲ Ask the children to find out which card has been used most/least often. Investigate for each card.
▲ Investigate how many additions become impossible when a card is 'lost'. Investigate for each card.
▲ Investigate different possible subtractions.

Answers

There are 16 possible additions.

1 + 2 = 3	1 + 8 = 9	3 + 4 = 7
1 + 3 = 4	2 + 3 = 5	3 + 5 = 8
1 + 4 = 5	2 + 4 = 6	3 + 6 = 9
1 + 5 = 6	2 + 5 = 7	4 + 5 = 9
1 + 6 = 7	2 + 6 = 8	
1 + 7 = 8	2 + 7 = 9	

Materials

▲ Outline of the addition drawn on paper/card
▲ Number line (1–10)
▲ Number cards (1–9)
(see photocopiable sheet on p.90)

Individual practice in Workbook 2a
Activity 1 Adding up

10

Card adding

You will need:
number cards (1–9)
a template

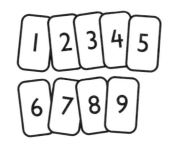

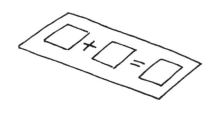

These additions have been made using three cards.
Make them on your template.

| 3 | + | 4 | = | 7 |

| 4 | + | 1 | = | 5 |

How many different additions can you make?
Record them here.

2

Activity

Sums or difference

Key vocabulary

sum
total
difference

Objectives

Understanding addition and subtraction
▲ Understand the operations of addition and subtraction

Rapid recall of addition and subtraction facts
▲ Know addition and subtraction facts for numbers to 12

Mental calculation strategies (subtraction)
▲ Find a small difference by counting up from the smaller to the larger number

Reasoning about numbers
▲ Explain methods and reasoning about numbers

Introducing the activity

▲ Practise finding the total when two dice are thrown, using a counting on strategy, with the number line as a model.
▲ Rehearse finding the difference between two dice throws, using the strategy of counting on from the smaller to the larger number.
▲ Discuss and record all the possible totals and differences when two dice are thrown.

Main activity

▲ Children should play the game in pairs. Explain the rules:
  • Player A uses the left-hand board, Player B the right-hand board.
  • Players take turns to throw the dice, and place a counter on their board on a number which is:
       either the **sum** (total) of the dice numbers
       or the **difference** between the dice numbers.
  • If a counter cannot be placed, do nothing.
  • The winner is the first player to completely cover his/her board with counters.

Developments

▲ The children make their own 5 × 3 board, choosing their own numbers to write in the squares. They can repeat the numbers if they wish. Encourage them to think strategically by asking: What are 'good' numbers to choose? Why?
▲ Design similar boards and play games which use differently numbered dice.

Materials

▲ Number line (1–20)
▲ Dice
▲ Counters

Individual practice in Workbook 2a
Activity 2 Totals and differences
Activity 2b More totals and differences

Sums or difference

You will need: two dice
counters

Player B

2	3	4	5	9
1	8	1	7	0
6	3	2	5	4

Player A

7	2	5	2	4
3	9	1	8	0
5	1	4	6	3

Find the T

Objectives

Counting and properties of numbers
▲ Count on or back in ones from any number
▲ Begin to count on in steps of 3, 4 or 5

Place value and ordering
▲ Read and write numbers to at least 100

Reasoning about numbers
▲ Recognise simple number patterns and predict

Introducing the activity

▲ Using squared paper, illustrate different ways of writing the numbers, in sequence, on a grid: along the rows, down the columns, left to right, right to left, top to bottom, bottom to top.
▲ Prepare different complete number grids. Hide individual numbers and sets of numbers (e.g. by covering them with cards, using Blu-tak). Ask the children to predict the hidden numbers. Remove the cards to check.

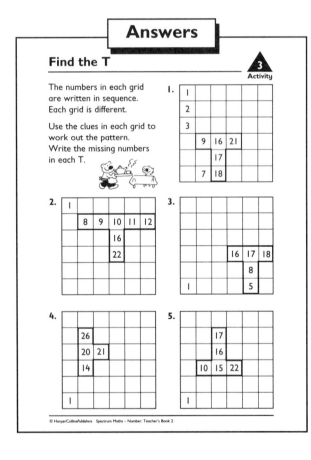

Main activity

▲ The children should test their predicted patterns on the grids, by counting, several times, before attempting to record the numbers in the T. Some children may want to write in the numbers outside the T.

Developments

▲ Children draw their own 6 × 6 grid, then draw a T shape, or some other shape. They decide on a rule for sequencing the numbers, and include one or two clues. After recording their own answer sheet, they could ask others to complete their grids.
▲ Extend to different sized grids, e.g. 8 × 8, or try rectangular grids.
▲ Create sequences which count in twos.
▲ Experiment with grids that use numbers following a spiral sequence.

Materials

▲ Squared paper
▲ Card
▲ Blu-tak

Individual practice in Workbook 2a
Activity 3 Missing numbers

Find the T

The numbers in each grid are written in sequence. Each grid is different.

Use the clues in each grid to work out the pattern. Write the missing numbers in each T.

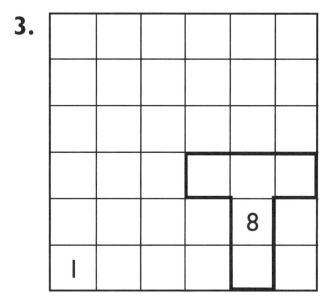

1.

1					
2					
3					
	9				
	7				

2.

1					
	9				

3.

				8	
1					

4.

	21				
1					

5.

	10				
1					

Dial numbers

Activity 4

Key vocabulary

pair
total

Objectives

Understanding addition and subtraction
▲ Understand the operation of addition, recognising that it can be done in any order
▲ Add more than two numbers, begin to add three single-digit numbers mentally

Rapid recall of addition and subtraction facts
▲ Know addition and subtraction facts for numbers to 10

Reasoning about numbers
▲ Solve a mathematical problem and recognise simple number patterns

Introducing the activity

▲ Illustrate the number pairs to ten by using ten pegs clipped to a coathanger. Place all the pegs to one side, then slide them, one at a time to the other side, showing the different number pairs by counting the number of pegs on each side, i.e. 10 and 0, then 9 and 1, then 8 and 2...

Answers

The different ways of revealing a total of ten with two dial numbers are:

(1, 9), (2, 8), (3, 7), (4, 6)

Ways of revealing a total of ten with three dial numbers are:

(0, 9, 1), (0, 8, 2), (0, 7, 3), (0, 6, 4)

(1, 7, 2), (1, 6, 3), (1, 5, 4), (2, 3, 5)

Main activity

▲ Encourage the children to record the pairs of numbers and to check they have found all the possible pairs. Repeat for sets of three numbers.

Developments

▲ Explore ways of revealing two or three dial numbers to make other totals.
▲ Develop children's mental awareness of the addition pairs to ten. Cover all the dial numbers with counters. Remove one counter and ask which counter should be removed to make a total of ten (or another total).
▲ Investigate sets of three dial numbers which add to 20.
▲ Draw a larger telephone dial on paper. Investigate drawing straight lines which join pairs of numbers that follow a given rule, e.g. 'have a total of ten'.

Materials

▲ Coathanger and ten pegs
▲ Counters

Individual practice in Workbook 2a
Activity 4 Telephone numbers

Dial numbers

You will need:

eight counters

Cover up eight dial numbers
with counters.
Leave two numbers which
add to 10.

Write down the pairs of
numbers which add to 10.

Now cover up seven numbers, leaving three which have a
total of 10.

Largest number game

Key vocabulary

largest
smallest
digit
2-digit
number
odd/even
nearest

Objectives

Place value and ordering

▲ Know the value of each digit in a 2-digit number

▲ Understand and use the vocabulary of comparing and ordering numbers

▲ Compare two or more 2-digit numbers, and say which is the largest

Reasoning about numbers

▲ Solve number puzzles

▲ Explain methods and reasoning about numbers

Introducing the activity

▲ Write a random selection of different 2-digit numbers on the board. Highlight any pair and ask which is the smaller, and which the larger. Use a 100 number square to help compare the two numbers. Repeat for several different pairs of numbers.

Main activity

▲ Children should play the game in pairs or threes. Explain the rules:

- Each player has a score sheet.
- One player throws the dice three times.
- After each throw, all players have to:
  either write the number in one of the two boxes available
  or say 'pass' and choose not to use the number. (Each player can pass only once in each round of three throws.)
- Once a number is written in a box it cannot be changed.
- The objective is to make the largest possible 2-digit number from the three throws.
- Score the rounds: two points for whoever has made the largest number in that round, one point for the next largest number.
- Players take turns to be the dice thrower.
- After eight rounds, the scores are added to find the winner.

Developments

▲ Change the objective: make the smallest number.

▲ Throw the dice four times and allow two passes.

▲ Change the objective to one of the following: largest/smallest odd number, largest/smallest even number.

▲ Change the objective to a 'nearness' target, e.g. nearest to 50, nearest to 35...

Materials

▲ 100 number square

▲ A dice

Individual practice in Workbook 2a
Activity 5 Largest and smallest

Largest number game

You will need:
a dice

score sheet

round 1   ☐ ☐   score ☐

round 2   ☐ ☐   score ☐

round 3   ☐ ☐   score ☐

round 4   ☐ ☐   score ☐

round 5   ☐ ☐   score ☐

round 6   ☐ ☐   score ☐

round 7   ☐ ☐   score ☐

round 8   ☐ ☐   score ☐

total ☐

Comparing pencils

Key
vocabulary

centimetre
length
longest
shortest
longer than
shorter than
first, second,
third...

Objectives

Place value and ordering
▲ Understand and use the vocabulary of ordering ordinal numbers (e.g. first, second...)
▲ Order a set of measures

Problems involving measures
▲ Use the vocabulary related to length (e.g. long, short...)
▲ Measure and compare lengths in centimetres

Data handling
▲ Represent and interpret data presented in a simple block graph and table

Introducing the activity

▲ The children start by colouring the pencils to match the stated colours. Then ask questions to help interpret the graph, and to encourage the use of appropriate language:
  • How many pencils are there altogether?
  • Which pencil is the longest? next longest?
  • Which pencil is the shortest? next shortest?
  • How long is the blue pencil? the red pencil?
  • Which pencil is 6 cm long? 3 cm long?
  • What colour pencils are longer than 6 cm?
  • What colour pencils are shorter than 5 cm?

Main activity

▲ Ask the children to make a list showing the length of each pencil.
▲ Encourage the children to use the list to answer questions of comparison, such as:
  • How much longer is the black pencil than the yellow pencil?
  • How much shorter is the white pencil than the purple pencil?
▲ Ask the children to write 'first', 'second', 'third' etc. alongside the longest, next longest etc.

Developments

▲ Measure the lengths of a set of pens and pencils to the nearest centimetre using a centimetre ruler (or the sheet for lengths up to 10 cm). Record their lengths in a table and help the children interpret the results.

Materials
▲ Coloured pencils
▲ Pens and pencils of different lengths
▲ Ruler

Individual practice in Workbook 2a
Activity 6 Height

Comparing pencils

Colour the pencils in the colours shown.

centimetres

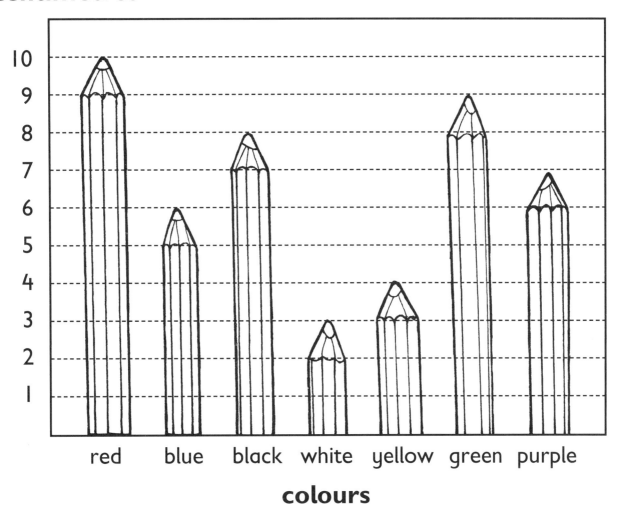

colours

See-saw numbers

Activity 7

Key vocabulary

add
total
balance

Objectives

Understanding addition and subtraction
▲ Understand the operation of addition and recognise that addition can be done in any order

Rapid recall of addition and subtraction facts
▲ Know addition facts for numbers to 10

Mental calculation strategies (addition)
▲ Use patterns of similar calculations

Reasoning about numbers
▲ Solve mathematical problems and recognise simple number patterns

Introducing the activity

▲ Draw a large see-saw, place two cards in position using Blu-tak and ask for the missing card. Use towers of interlocking cubes to aid as a check. For example, for balancing 8, make a tower of eight, and break it into two smaller towers.
▲ Discuss whether 7 above 3 on the right of a see-saw is the same as 3 above 7. It is simpler to assume that they are the same.
▲ Point out that, for the purpose of this activity, the numbers on the right must be two different numbers, as there is only one card available of each number to 10.

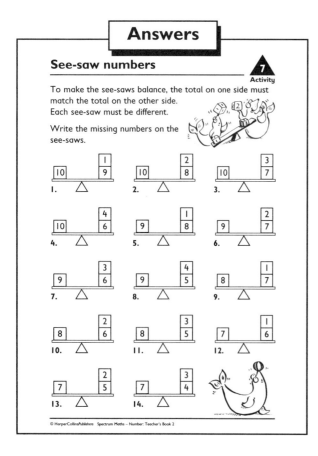

Main activity

▲ Prepare a large outline of a see-saw for the children to use with the number cards, to help them find the balancing numbers before they write them down.

Developments

▲ Investigate how many different ways there are of balancing each of the numbers from 1 to 10. Do this for both allowing and disallowing repeat numbers.
▲ Extend to using numbers greater than 10.
▲ Extend to see-saws which have three numbers on one side to balance one number on the other side.

Materials

▲ Number cards (1–10) (see photocopiable sheet on p.90)
▲ Blu-tak
▲ See-saw paper (see photocopiable sheet on p.91)

Individual practice in Workbook 2a
Activity 7 Balance the numbers

See-saw numbers

To make the see-saws balance, the total on one side must match the total on the other side. Each see-saw must be different.

Write the missing numbers on the see-saws.

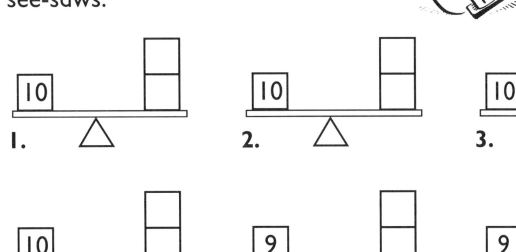

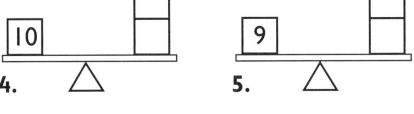

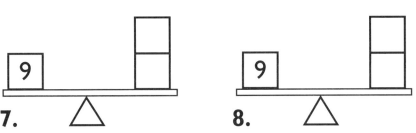

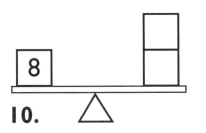

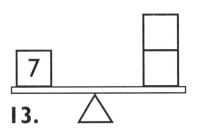

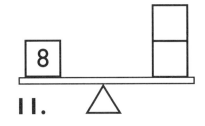

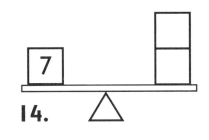

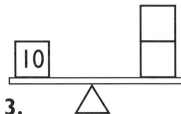

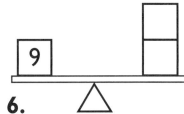

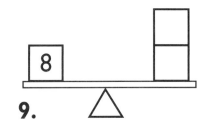

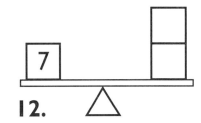

Clock game

Objectives

Problems involving measures

▲ To read the time to the hour, half-hour and quarter-hour on an analogue clock
▲ To use the vocabulary related to time

Introducing the activity

▲ Use two paper circles (or paper plates), each a different colour. Cut a straight line from the edge to the centre of each. Intersect the two circles at the cut lines. Keeping one circle firm, rotate the other to demonstrate quarter turns, half turns, etc. Demonstrate the amount of turn needed for 'quarter past', 'half past' and 'quarter to' times.

▲ Use a clockface with movable hands to demonstrate different 'o'clock' times, proceeding to 'half past' times, 'quarter past' times and 'quarter to' times. Write different times on the board in words. Choose children to rotate the hands to show the times on the clock.

Main activity

▲ Make 20 time cards, with 'quarter to', 'quarter past' and 'half past' times written in words, from 'quarter to 1' to 'quarter past 7'.
▲ Children play the clock game in pairs. Explain the rules:
 • Shuffle the time cards and place them in a pile, face down.
 • Each player reveals the top card in turns, reading the time aloud and placing a counter on the matching clock on the sheet.
 • The children check each other's moves.
 • The winner is the first player to have three of his/her counters in a straight line in any direction.

Developments

▲ Shuffle the cards and deal them out equally. Players look at their hand and select which card to play in turns. The first player to have four counters in a straight line wins.
▲ Cut out the clocks from the sheet and order them, starting with 'quarter to 1'.
▲ Use the time cards placed face down. One child reveals a card, and all participants have to draw hands on a blank clock face to show the matching time.
▲ Create a new sheet of digital clocks with the same times. Play the game again, using the same time cards.

Materials

▲ Two sets of counters
▲ 20 time cards

Individual practice in Workbook 2a
Activity 8 Quarter-hours

Clock game

You will need: a set of counters each
20 time cards

Take away game

Key
vocabulary

dice
take away
subtract
hexagon

Objectives

Understanding addition and subtraction

▲ Understand the operation of subtraction as 'take away'
▲ Recognise that subtraction is the inverse of addition

Rapid recall of addition and subtraction facts

▲ Know subtraction facts for numbers to 10

Mental calculation strategies (subtraction)

▲ Put the larger number first and count back in ones
▲ Find a small difference by counting up from the smaller to the larger number

Introducing the activity

▲ Practise subtracting from 10, using a set of number cards (1–9). Reveal the cards, one at a time, asking the children to subtract the number from 10. Use a number line as a model to illustrate.
▲ Encourage the children to see the links between addition and subtraction, i.e. '10 take away 7' is the same as finding what must be added to 7 to make 10.
▲ Discuss the shape of the cells on the playing board.

Main activity

▲ Children should play the game in pairs. Explain the rules:
  • Players take turns to throw the dice, then subtract the dice number from 10.
  • If possible, the player places a counter on a matching hexagon on the board.
  • Only one counter is allowed on each hexagon.
  • If a counter cannot be placed, do nothing.
  • When all the hexagons have been covered, the winner is the player who has placed the most counters.

Developments

▲ Subtract from a number other than 10, e.g. 9 or 11.
▲ Use a dice numbered differently, e.g. a blank cube numbered 6, 7, 8, 9, 10, 11 and subtract from 15 each time.
▲ Investigate how many of each number appear on the board.
▲ Link the activity to finding change from 10p.

Materials

▲ Number cards (1–9) (see photocopiable sheet on p.90)
▲ Number line (1–10)
▲ A dice
▲ Counters

Individual practice in Workbook 2a
Activity 9 Taking away
Activity 9b More taking away

Take away game

You will need: a dice
counters

Activity

Split the strip

Key vocabulary

add
addition

Objectives

Understanding addition and subtraction
▲ Understand the operation of addition
▲ Begin to add three single-digit numbers mentally

Rapid recall of addition and subtraction facts
▲ Know addition facts for numbers to 10

Mental calculation strategies (addition)
▲ Add three small numbers by putting the largest first

Reasoning about numbers
▲ Solve mathematical problems and recognise simple patterns
▲ Explain methods and reasoning about numbers

Introducing the activity

▲ Start by splitting a strip of eight cubes into two pieces. Write down all of the different pairs for the children to see (1 + 7, 2 + 6, 3 + 5 etc.).
▲ Discuss whether 3 + 5 is the same as 5 + 3. Assume that it is for the purpose of this activity.
▲ Discuss whether 0 + 8 is allowed.
▲ Hide a tower of eight cubes behind your back, break it into two, then reveal one part. Ask the children to tell you how many cubes are in the hidden section.
▲ Extend to splitting into two using different lengths of starting strips.

Answers

The strip of eight cubes can be split in the following different ways.

☐ ☐ ☐☐☐☐☐☐ (1, 1, 6)

☐ ☐☐ ☐☐☐☐☐ (1, 2, 5)

☐ ☐☐☐ ☐☐☐☐ (1, 3, 4)

☐☐ ☐☐ ☐☐☐☐ (2, 2, 4)

☐☐ ☐☐☐ ☐☐☐ (2, 3, 3)

Main activity

▲ Encourage the children to take care not to repeat an arrangement, i.e. 1 + 2 + 5 is the same as 1 + 5 + 2.
▲ Discuss ways of recording the splits, e.g. by drawing the arrangements on squared paper, or by writing them as additions, e.g. 1 + 1 + 6.

Developments

▲ Investigate how many splits have two parts the same size, e.g. 2 + 2 + 4.
▲ Extend to splitting strips of different lengths.
▲ Extend to splitting strips into four.

Materials

▲ Interlocking cubes
▲ Squared paper

Individual practice in Workbook 2a
Activity 10 Adding three numbers

Split the strip

You will need: interlocking cubes

Join eight cubes to make
a strip like this.

Here are two ways of splitting the strip into three.

$1 + 2 + 5 = 8$

$4 + 2 + 2 = 8$

Find different ways of splitting the strip into three.
Record them here.

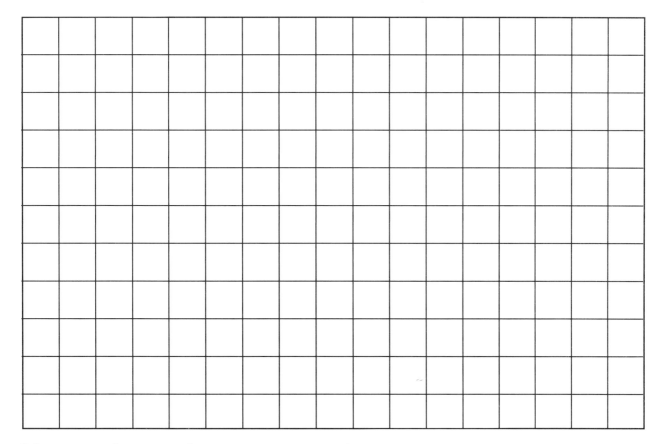

You might need more squared paper.

Activity

Ice cream

Key vocabulary

block graph
pictogram
popular
most/least
more/fewer

Objectives

Data handling

▲ Collect, represent and interpret data in pictograms and block graphs

Introducing the activity

▲ Ask the children to colour the ice creams and blocks to match the colours of the different flavours.

▲ Discuss the pictogram and the block graph shown on the sheet. Point out that a graph should have a title, and that the axes of the block graph must both be clearly labelled.

▲ Ask questions to help interpret the graphs:
- How many children voted for strawberry? mint...?
- Which flavour was the most popular? second most popular...?
- Which flavour was the least popular? second least popular...?
- How many children voted altogether?
- How many more prefer chocolate to mint?
- How many fewer prefer mint to vanilla?
- How many prefer either strawberry or vanilla?
- How many did not vote for mint?

Main activity

▲ Discuss different flavours of ice cream. Decide on a list of not more than five.

▲ Groups of children collect data on their favourite flavour of ice cream, then draw both a pictogram and a block graph (using block graph paper) to show the results.

▲ Draw another block graph which combines the results of the groups.

Developments

▲ Collect data based on preferences for some other item, e.g. colour, flavour of crisp, fruit...

▲ Extend the drawing of pictograms to include one symbol representing two votes.

Materials

▲ Block graph paper (see photocopiable sheet on p.92)

Individual practice in Workbook 2a
Activity 11 Block graph

Ice cream

Our favourite ice cream flavour

vanilla	🍦 🍦 🍦 🍦
strawberry	🍦 🍦 🍦
chocolate	🍦 🍦 🍦 🍦 🍦 🍦
mint	🍦 🍦

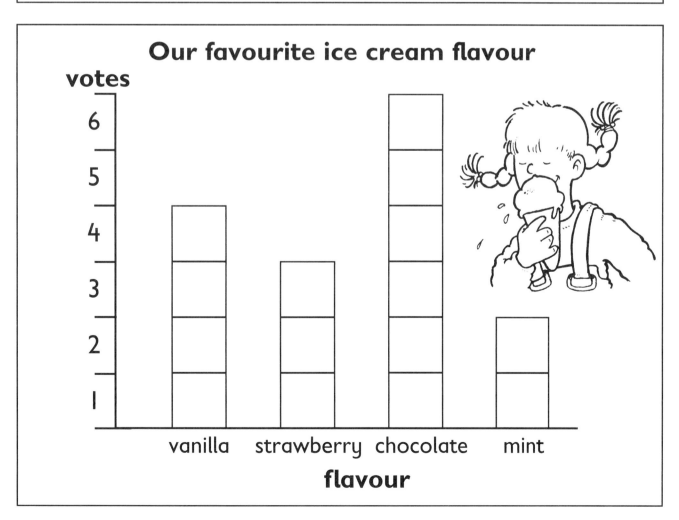

Our favourite ice cream flavour

Three coins

Key vocabulary

coin
total
value
amount
change

Objectives

Understanding addition and subtraction
▲ Understand the operation of addition
▲ Add more than two numbers

Mental calculation strategies (addition)
▲ Add three small numbers by putting the largest first and/or find a pair totalling 10
▲ Use known number facts to add mentally

Reasoning about numbers
▲ Solve mathematical problems

Problems involving 'real life' or money
▲ Use mental addition to solve money problems, including finding totals up to 30p, and give change
▲ Recognise coins and begin to use £.p notation

Introducing the activity

▲ Clarify recognition of the different coins with the children.
▲ Demonstrate and practise adding two coins, then three coins, by starting with the larger valued coin, then adding the remainder. Use a number line to check.

Answers

Below are some examples of making the amounts to 30p. Some amounts can be made in more than one way.

1p	16p (10, 5, 1)
2p	17p (10, 5, 2)
3p (1, 1, 1)	18p
4p (1, 1, 2)	19p
5p (1, 2, 2)	20p (10, 5, 5)
6p (2, 2, 2)	21p (10, 10, 1)
7p (5, 1, 1)	22p (10, 10, 2)
8p (5, 2, 1)	23p
9p (5, 2, 2)	24p
10p	25p (10, 10, 5)
11p (5, 5, 1)	26p
12p (5, 5, 2)	27p
13p (10, 2, 1)	28p
14p (10, 2, 2)	29p
15p (5, 5, 5)	30p (10, 10, 10)

Main activity

▲ Discuss how the amounts can be recorded, e.g. by drawing round coins, using sticky circles, using rubber coin stamps. Alternatively, the amounts could be written as additions, e.g. 10p + 2p + 2p = 14p.

Developments

▲ Investigate which amounts can be made in more than one way, e.g. 10p, 1p, 1p = 12p = 5p, 5p, 2p.
▲ Investigate which amounts cannot be made with three coins.
▲ Investigate the change for each amount from 20p, then 30p.
▲ Try introducing other coins, e.g. 20p, 50p.
▲ Try using four coins for the additions.

Materials

▲ Coins of different values (including at least 1p, 2p, 5p,10p)
▲ Number line (1–30)
▲ Sticky circles or rubber coin stamps

Individual practice in Workbook 2a
Activity 12 Coin totals

Three coins

You need sets of these coins.

These three coins make different amounts.

   makes 12p

   makes 9p

What different amounts can you make with three coins?
Record your answers here.
Use another sheet of paper if you need to.

Spot the difference

Objectives

Understanding addition and subtraction
▲ Understand the operation of subtraction as 'difference'

Rapid recall of addition and subtraction facts
▲ Know subtraction facts for numbers to 10

Mental calculation strategies (subtraction)
▲ Find a difference by counting up from the smaller to the larger number

Reasoning about numbers
▲ Solve mathematical problems and recognise simple number patterns
▲ Investigate general statements about numbers

Introducing the activity

▲ Consolidate the idea of 'difference' using towers of interlocking cubes. To help the children to find the difference between 6 and 4, say, make a 6-tower and a 4-tower and discuss the difference, by counting on from the shorter to the taller tower.
▲ Practise finding the difference between two dice throws, or the difference between the numbers of spots on each side of a domino.

Answers

The differences 0–5 are possible in the following ways.

0 | 6 6 | 5 5 | 4 4 | 3 3 | 2 2 | 1 1 |

1 | 6 5 | 5 4 | 4 3 | 3 2 | 2 1 |

2 | 6 4 | 5 3 | 4 2 | 3 1 |

3 | 6 3 | 5 2 | 4 1 |

4 | 6 2 | 5 1 |

5 | 6 1 |

Main activity

▲ Discuss how the pairs are to be recorded, e.g. by drawing spots, or by writing numbers.

6 − 3   5 − 2   4 − 1

6 3   5 2   4 1

Developments

▲ Investigate what differences are possible for a given dice total. For example, for a total of 8, then it is possible to have a difference of 4 (6, 2), a difference of 2 (5, 3), and a difference of 0 (4, 4).
▲ Repeat the activities, but with dice numbered differently, e.g. by writing 3, 4, 5, 6, 7, 8 on the faces of two blank cubes.
▲ Using number cards (1–10 or 1–20), investigate ways of making differences.

Materials

▲ Interlocking cubes
▲ Dice
▲ Dominoes
▲ Number cards (1–10 or 1–20) (see photocopiable sheet on p.90)

Individual practice in Workbook 2a
Activity 13 Find the difference

Spot the difference

You will need:
two dice

These throws have a difference of 3.

Find different pairs which have a difference of 2.
Record your work here.

Can you find any other differences?

14

Activity

2-digit numbers

Key
vocabulary

2-digit
number
units digit
tens digit
larger
smaller
largest
smallest
first,
second...

Objectives

Place value and ordering

▲ Read and write 2-digit numbers

▲ Know the value of each digit in a 2-digit number

▲ Understand and use the vocabulary of comparing and ordering 2-digit numbers, including ordinal numbers

▲ Compare two or more 2-digit numbers, and say which is the largest

▲ Order a set of 1- and 2-digit numbers

Reasoning about numbers

▲ Solve mathematical problems and recognise simple number patterns

▲ Investigate a general statement about numbers and find examples to satisfy it

Introducing the activity

▲ Discuss the word 'digit'. Help the children to recognise the tens digit in 2-digit numbers, as well as the units digit.

▲ Compare two 2-digit numbers to see which has the larger tens digit, and subsequently discuss which is the larger and smaller of the two numbers. Practise locating the position of numbers on a 100 division number line.

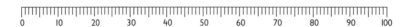

```
0    10   20   30   40   50   60   70   80   90   100
```

Answers

The 2-digit numbers that contain the digit 4 are:

14, 24, 34, 40, 41, 42, 43, 44, 45, 46, 47, 48, 49, 54, 64, 74, 84, 94

The 2-digit numbers that contain the digit 7 are:

17, 27, 37, 47, 57, 67, 70, 71, 72, 73, 74, 75, 76, 77, 78, 79, 87, 97

Main activity

▲ Encourage the children to complete the sheet. Emphasise that the digit 4 can either be in the tens place or the units place, or both. A systematic approach would consider, for example, all numbers with 4 in the units place first, then the tens place.

Developments

▲ It is possible to find 18 different 2-digit numbers which contain the digit 4, and 18 which contain the digit 7. Investigate whether there are 18 different 2-digit numbers for each of the other digits.

▲ Consolidate the ordinal numbers, by asking questions about the ordered lists:
  • Which is the third in the list?
  • Which is fifteenth?
  • What position is 47?

▲ Extend to 3-digit numbers.

Materials

▲ Number line (1–100)

Individual practice in Workbook 2a
Activity 14 Ordering

2-digit numbers

Each of these 2-digit numbers has the digit 3 in it.

| 23 | 37 | 83 | 33 |

Write 18 different 2-digit numbers which all have the digit 4 in them.

Now write them in order from smallest to largest.

How many 2-digit numbers can you write which have a digit 7 in them?

Activity 15

Train numbers

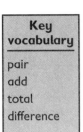

Key vocabulary

pair
add
total
difference

Objectives

Understanding addition and subtraction

▲ Understand the operations of addition and subtraction
▲ Begin to recognise that subtraction is the inverse of addition

Rapid recall of addition and subtraction facts

▲ Know addition facts for pairs of numbers to 12

Mental calculation strategies (addition)

▲ Say the subtraction fact corresponding to a given addition fact

Introducing the activity

▲ Practise recognition of addition bonds, e.g. to illustrate bonds to 10, break towers of ten interlocking cubes into two smaller towers in different ways.
▲ Practise recall of the facts by placing the tower of ten behind your back, breaking it into two, revealing one of the smaller towers and asking the children to predict the size of the other tower.

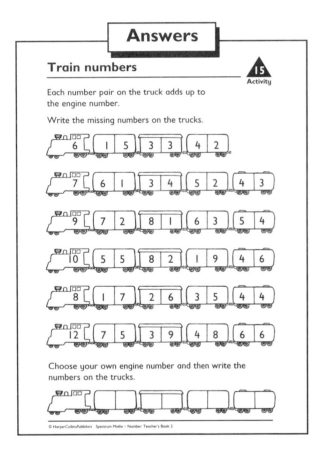

Main activity

▲ Before the children attempt the sheet, discuss the fact that for the purpose of this activity 3, 7 and 7, 3 are the same pair, and therefore do not require separate trucks.

Developments

▲ Investigate how many different trucks can be pulled by different numbered engines.
▲ Investigate truck numbers for larger engine numbers.
▲ Build trains for which the differences between the pairs of truck numbers match the engine numbers.

Materials

▲ Interlocking cubes

Individual practice in Workbook 2a
Activity 15 Number pairs

Train numbers

Each number pair on the truck adds up to the engine number.

Write the missing numbers on the trucks.

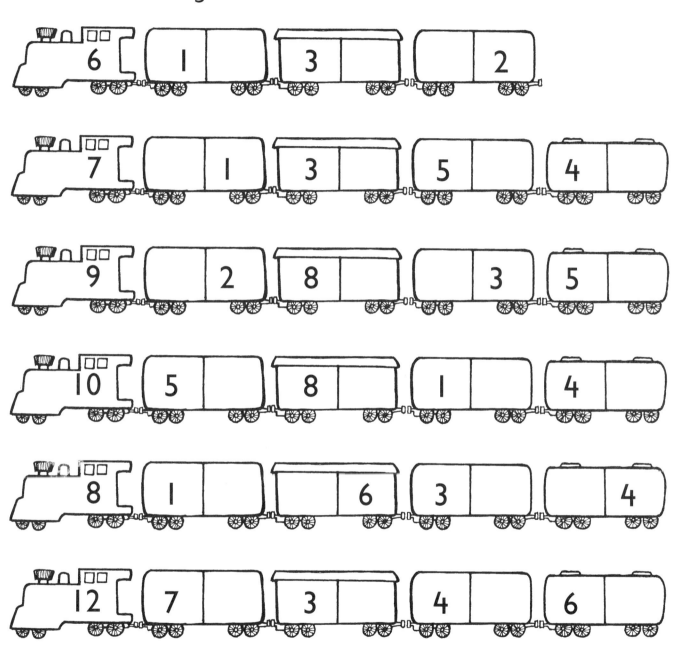

Choose your own engine number and then write the numbers on the trucks.

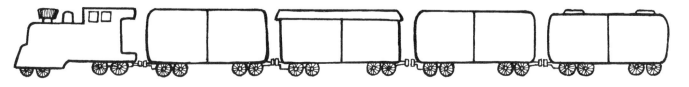

Twos

Key vocabulary

2-digit number
largest
smallest
units digit
units place
tens digit
tens place
round

Objectives

Place value and ordering
▲ Read and write numbers to 100
▲ Know the value of each digit in a 2-digit number
▲ Understand and use the vocabulary of comparing and ordering 2-digit numbers
▲ Compare two or more 2-digit numbers, and say which is the largest
▲ Order a set of 2-digit numbers

Estimating and rounding
▲ Begin to round a 2-digit number to its nearest 10

Reasoning about numbers
▲ Solve a mathematical problem, recognising simple patterns and predict
▲ Investigate general statements about number (e.g. 'Twelve different 2-digit numbers can be made from four different digits')

Introducing the activity

▲ Consolidate the meaning of 'digit' by asking the children to describe which are the tens and units digits in 2-digit numbers.
▲ Provide practice in creating 2-digit numbers using number cards (1–9). Ask the children, for example, to make the number which has 3 as its units digit and 7 as its tens digit. Read the number together.
▲ Compare two 2-digit numbers to see which has the larger tens digit, leading to discussion on which is the larger and smaller of the two numbers. Practise locating their position on a 100 division number line or on a 100 square.

Answers

The 12 different 2-digit numbers in order are:

12, 14, 15, 21, 24, 25,

41, 42, 45, 51, 52, 54

Main activity

▲ After the children have tried the activity, discuss ways of working systematically, e.g. start by making all the 2-digit numbers which have a 1 in the tens place, then those with 2 in the tens place etc.

Developments

▲ Choose a different set of four cards and repeat the activity. Start by predicting whether or not there will be 12 possible answers as before.
▲ Investigate what happens if two of the four cards are identical.
▲ Investigate how many of the 2-digit numbers contain a particular digit.
▲ Repeat the activity with three cards only, or try with five cards.
▲ Round each number to its nearest 10.
▲ Which of the 2-digit numbers is nearest to 10, to 20, to 30…?

Materials

▲ Number cards (1–9) (see photocopiable sheet on p.90)
▲ Number line (1–100) or a 100 square

Individual practice in Workbook 2a
Activity 16 Tens and units

Twos

You will need:
four number cards

Two of the cards have been placed together to make the number 24.

2 4

Put other pairs of cards together to make 2-digit numbers.
How many different 2-digit numbers can you make?
Record them here.

Now write them in order from smallest to largest.

Doubling machine

Activity

Key vocabulary

double
half
halve
table
odd/even

Objectives

Understanding multiplication and division

▲ Understand the operation of multiplication as repeated addition

▲ Recognise halving as the inverse of doubling

Rapid recall of multiplication and division facts

▲ Know or derive quickly doubles of all numbers to 12, and the corresponding halves

Introducing the activity

▲ Consolidate the idea of doubles through addition, e.g. 'double 4' is 4 + 4.

▲ Use towers of interlocking cubes to illustrate 'double 4'. Join two 4-towers together to make an 8-tower.

▲ Consolidate the idea of halving by reversing the process.

Answers

double

in	3	5	6	8	9	12
out	6	10	12	16	18	24

half

in	2	8	4	20	14	22
out	1	4	2	10	7	11

Main activity

▲ Discuss the difference between the tables for the 'doubling' machine and the 'halving' machine.

▲ Discuss the oddness and evenness of the numbers coming out of both machines.

Developments

▲ Investigate what happens if different coins are put through the machines. Is there an equivalent coin for each answer? Can the answers be made up of a number of coins?

▲ What happens when odd numbers are put into the 'halving' machine?

▲ Ask the children to devise their own machines using a combination of different functions.

Materials

▲ Interlocking cubes

Individual practice in Workbook 2a
Activity 17 Doubling and halving

Doubling machine

This is a **doubling** machine.
When a number is put **in**,
out comes its **double**.

When 3 is put **in**, **out** comes 6.

Complete this table for
the doubling machine.

in	3	5	6	8	9	12
out	6					

This is a **halving** machine.

Complete this table for
the halving machine.

in						
out	1	4	2	10	7	11

Write down numbers of your own to go into these
machines and complete the tables.

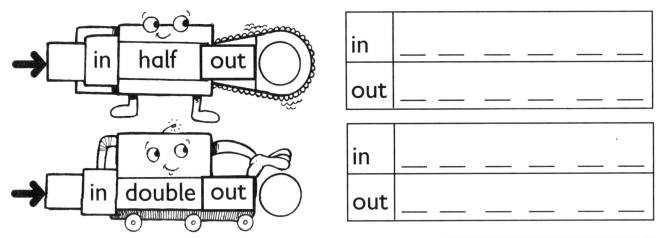

in	_ _ _ _ _ _
out	_ _ _ _ _ _

in	_ _ _ _ _ _
out	_ _ _ _ _ _

Guess the number

Activity

Key vocabulary

more/less
between
greater
odd/even
multiple

Objectives

Counting and properties of numbers
▲ Begin to recognise multiples of 2, 5 or 10

Place value and ordering
▲ Know the value of each digit in a 2-digit number
▲ Understand and use the vocabulary of comparing and ordering 2-digit numbers

Reasoning about numbers
▲ Solve mathematical puzzles
▲ Explain methods and reasoning about numbers orally

Introducing the activity
▲ Consolidate the children's understanding associated with the language and comparison of number, e.g. clarify that 'more than 45' does not include 45.
▲ Discuss odd and even 2-digit numbers and their properties.

Main activity
▲ Play the game as a class. Explain the rules:
  • One person is chosen to 'think of a number' that appears on the grid.
  • Everyone else asks questions to try and deduce the number, e.g. Is it an odd number? Is it more than 20? Is it between 30 and 50?
  • The 'chooser' may only answer 'yes' or 'no'.
  • Count how many questions are needed to deduce the number as the game progresses and try to better this each time.
▲ Organise the children to play the game in pairs. One member of the pair thinks of the number, whilst the other tries to deduce it. Encourage the children to keep a record of the questions and answers.

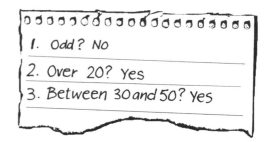

1. Odd? No
2. Over 20? Yes
3. Between 30 and 50? Yes

Developments
▲ Reduce the range of possible numbers, e.g. cover half the sheet.
▲ Extend the range of numbers to include 3-digit numbers.
▲ Player A describes the number without naming it. B tries to guess after each piece of information.

Individual practice in Workbook 2a
Activity 18 Clues

Guess the number

1	2	3	4	5	6	7	8	9	10
11	12	13	14	15	16	17	18	19	20
21	22	23	24	25	26	27	28	29	30
31	32	33	34	35	36	37	38	39	40
41	42	43	44	45	46	47	48	49	50
51	52	53	54	55	56	57	58	59	60
61	62	63	64	65	66	67	68	69	70
71	72	73	74	75	76	77	78	79	80
81	82	83	84	85	86	87	88	89	90
91	92	93	94	95	96	97	98	99	100

Colouring fractions

Activity 19

Objectives

Fractions

▲ Recognise, name and find one half and one quarter of shapes

▲ Begin to recognise that two halves or four quarters make one whole and that two quarters are equal to one half

Introducing the activity

▲ Illustrate halves to the children by folding a sheet of paper. Fold again to show quarters.

▲ Clarify that the shape has to be split into *equal* parts to make true halves and quarters.

▲ Extend to folding different regular shapes into halves and quarters.

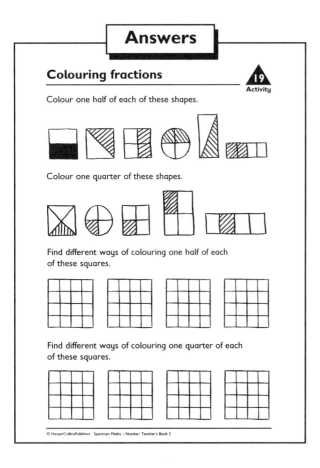

Main activity

▲ Before the children start the sheet, discuss the fact that, for some shapes shown, there are a number of different correct ways of showing halves and quarters.

▲ You might like to provide the children with paper shapes to help them complete the sheet.

Developments

▲ Extend to colouring other fractions, e.g. thirds, fifths and tenths using outlines drawn on squared paper.

▲ Discuss the fractions of the shapes which are *not* coloured on each shape.

Materials

▲ Squared paper
▲ Paper rectangles, squares, circles

Individual practice in Workbook 2a
Activity 19 Fractions

Colouring fractions

Colour one half of each of these shapes.

Colour one quarter of these shapes.

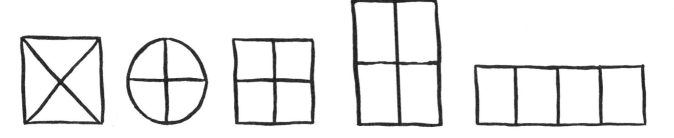

Find different ways of colouring one half of each of these squares.

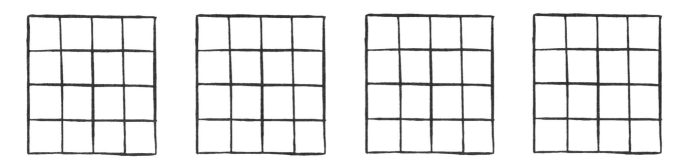

Find different ways of colouring one quarter of each of these squares.

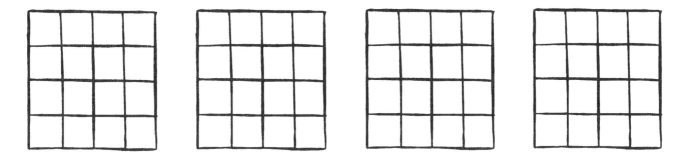

Number pairs

Key vocabulary

pair
total
add
table
pattern
odd/even

Objectives

Understanding addition and subtraction
▲ Understand the operation of addition and use the related vocabulary

Rapid recall of addition and subtraction facts
▲ Know addition facts for all numbers to 10
▲ Know pairs of numbers with a total of 20

Mental calculation strategies (addition)
▲ Bridge through 10, then adjust

Reasoning about numbers
▲ Solve mathematical problems and recognise simple number patterns

Introducing the activity

▲ Start with one set of number cards each (1–10). Ask the children to create pairs of cards with a total of 6: (1, 5) and (2, 4). Extend this to pairs which total 7, then 8, and so on.

Answers

The five different pairs which total 12 are:

1, 11   2, 10   3, 9   4, 8   5, 7

The number of possible pairs for other totals are:

total	5	6	7	8	9	10	11	12
number of pairs	2	2	3	3	4	4	5	5
total	13	14	15	16	17	18	19	20
number of pairs	6	6	7	7	8	8	9	9

Main activity

▲ Discuss ways of recording the pairs. Two possibilities include:

total 12	or
1, 11	1 + 11 = 12
2, 10	2 + 10 = 12

Developments

▲ Try to make all totals from 1–20 using pairs of cards. Record the results in a table. Can the children spot any pattern?
▲ Investigate how many pairs are made from two odd numbers and two even numbers.
▲ Extend to totals greater than 20.
▲ Change the set of number cards, e.g. to 1–15.

Materials

▲ Number cards (1–20) (see photocopiable sheet on p.90)

Individual practice in Workbook 2a
Activity 20 Pairs
Activity 20b Pairs to 20

Number pairs

You will need:

number cards (1–20)

This pair of number cards totals 12.

| 10 | 2 |

Find as many different pairs as you can which total 12.
Record your answers here.

Find pairs which have other totals.

21

Activity

Guess the length

Key vocabulary

length
long
centimetre
measure
difference
estimate

Objectives

Understanding addition and subtraction
▲ Understand the operation of subtraction as 'difference' and the related vocabulary

Estimating and rounding
▲ Understand and use the vocabulary of estimation

Problems involving measures
▲ Use the vocabulary related to length, estimate and measure lengths in centimetres, using a ruler

Data handling
▲ Collect and represent data in simple tables

Introducing the activity

▲ Demonstrate how to use a ruler to measure lengths, with the start of the scale on the ruler (0 cm) lining up exactly with the end of the line being measured.
▲ Make a set of strips of card whose lengths are whole numbers of centimetres. Help the children practise estimating their lengths by relating them to a 10 centimetre strip. Then use the ruler to check their estimates.

Answers

The lines have the following measurements:

a	=	13 cm	f	=	10 cm
b	=	5 cm	g	=	9 cm
c	=	8 cm	h	=	4 cm
d	=	7 cm	i	=	5 cm
e	=	13 cm	j	=	12 cm

Main activity

▲ Children work in pairs. Explain the rules:
  • Player A estimates the length of line a (all the lines have lengths which are whole numbers of centimetres), without reference to the ruler.
  • Player A records his/her estimate in the table below (in the 'estimate' column).
  • Repeat for Player B.
  • Players then measure the length of the line, and record it in the 'length' column.
  • Players then calculate the difference between the estimate and the length and record it in the 'difference' column.
  • The winner is the player with the least total difference.

Developments

▲ The player whose estimate is the closest for each line wins that round. Who wins the most rounds?
▲ Draw a different set of lines, including some longer lines, and play again.
▲ Draw triangles with sides which are whole numbers of centimetres. Estimate, then measure the total length of the three sides, i.e. its perimeter.

Materials

▲ Rulers marked in centimetres
▲ A 10 centimetre strip

Individual practice in Workbook 2b
Activity 21 Centimetres

Guess the length

You will need: a ruler marked in centimetres

```
0  1  2  3  4  5  6  7  8  9  10
          centimetres
```

a.

b.

c.

d.

e.

f.

g.

h.

i.

j.

line	length	Player A		Player B	
		estimate	difference	estimate	difference
a					
b					
c					
d					
e					
f					
g					
h					
i					
j					
	total		**total**		

22 Largest odd, smallest even

Key vocabulary

digit
2-digit
number
largest
smallest
odd/even
units digit
tens digit

Objectives

Counting and properties of numbers
▲ Recognise odd and even 2-digit numbers

Place value and ordering
▲ Know the value of each digit in a 2-digit number
▲ Understand and use the vocabulary of comparing and ordering 2-digit numbers
▲ Compare two 2-digit numbers, and say which is the largest

Introducing the activity

▲ Provide the children with sets of number cards (1–9), and ask them to select three cards, e.g. 4, 7, 2. With these three cards they should try to make different 2-digit numbers. Discuss whether the numbers they make are odd or even. If necessary, discuss the units digits of odd and even numbers. Chant them in sequence to reveal patterns in the units digits.

▲ Using the same three cards, make different even 2-digit numbers (24, 42, 72, 74). Which is the smallest? (24). Make different odd 2-digit numbers (27, 47). Which is the largest? (47).

Answers

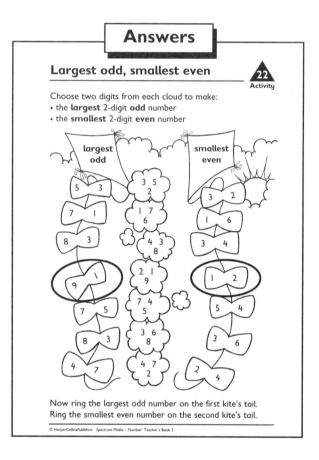

Main activity

▲ The children could use number cards to help them complete the sheet. Then ask them to ring the largest odd number from the kite's tail, and also the smallest even number.

Developments

▲ Ask the children to find the largest even and the smallest odd number they can make from three chosen cards.
▲ Extend to using four number cards instead of three.
▲ Investigate patterns in the number of possible odd numbers and even numbers that can be made when the three digits are: all even, one even and two odd, two even and one odd, all odd.

Materials

▲ Number cards (1–9) (see photocopiable sheet on p.90)

Individual practice in Workbook 2b
Activity 22 Large, small, odd, even

Largest odd, smallest even

Choose two digits from each cloud to make:
- the **largest** 2-digit **odd** number
- the **smallest** 2-digit **even** number

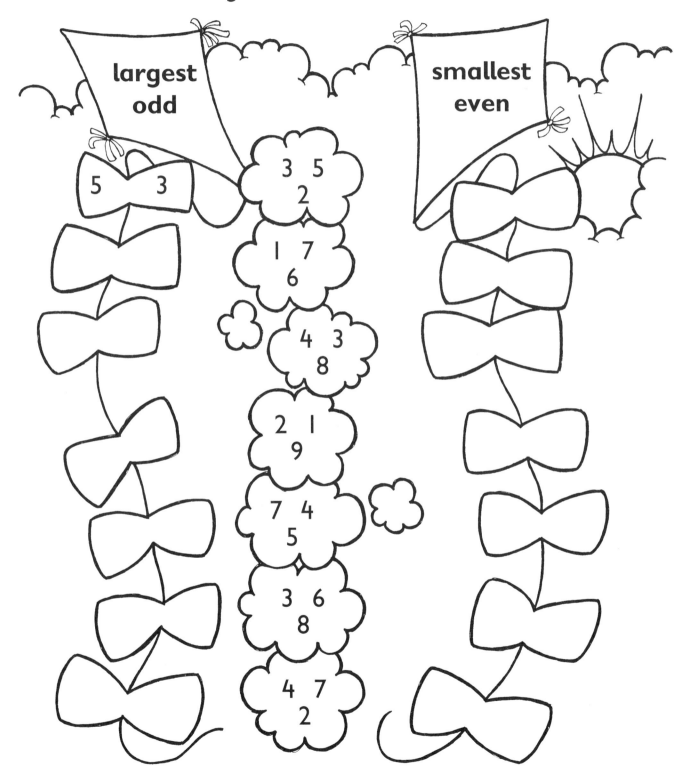

Now ring the largest odd number on the first kite's tail.
Ring the smallest even number on the second kite's tail.

23

Activity

Jumping

Key vocabulary

forwards
backwards
odd/even

Objectives

Counting and properties of numbers

▲ Count on in twos from and back to zero and recognise odd and even numbers
▲ Count on or back in steps of 3 or 4
▲ Begin to recognise multiples of 2

Understanding multiplication and division

▲ Understand the operations of multiplication and division, through repeated jumps on a number line

Introducing the activity

▲ Starting at 0, count along the number line on the sheet in twos, pointing to each number in turn and saying the number aloud. With the children, chant the numbers in sequence. Extend to reciting the numbers backwards.
▲ Ask the children to predict the number you will land on after four jumps of two, two jumps, ten jumps etc.
▲ Ask the children to predict how many jumps are needed to land on 16, for example.

Main activity

▲ The activity is designed initially to increase children's awareness of odd and even numbers up to 31. When the children have completed the sheet, discuss the patterns in the units digits of odd and even numbers.
▲ The completed table will contain even numbers (in the 'yes' column) and odd numbers (in the 'no' column).

Developments

▲ Extend to jumping in units other than two, e.g. three, five...
▲ Ask the children to investigate which numbers they need to start on in order to finish on 0 when jumping backwards in fives, in tens, in threes...
▲ Extend the activity to include larger numbers than 31. Use, for example, a 100 number square.

Materials

▲ Counters
▲ A 100 number square

Individual practice in Workbook 2b
Activity 23 What's next?

54

Jumping

You will need: counters

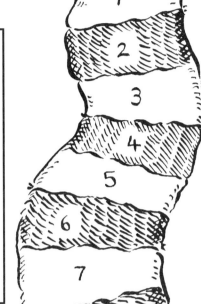

Place a counter on 16.
Jump in twos, back along the line towards 0.
Do you finish on 0?
Write 16 under **yes** or **no**
in the table.

Do this again, starting with
different numbers.

yes	no
16	

Number words

Key vocabulary

block graph
more/fewer

Objectives

Place value and ordering

▲ Read and write the numbers to 10 in words

▲ Say the number that is 1 more or less than a given number

Data handling

▲ Collect, represent and interpret data in a block graph

Introducing the activity

▲ Make some number word cards for the numbers from one to ten.

▲ Show them randomly to the children and ask them to tell you:
  • the number
  • how many letters there are in the number word
  • the number 'one more' and 'one less'
  • the number 'two more' and 'two less'.

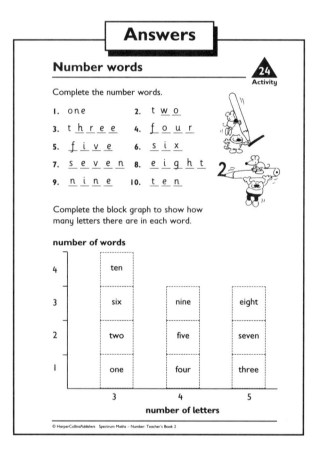

Answers

Number words

Complete the number words.

1. o n e   2. t w o
3. t h r e e   4. f o u r
5. f i v e   6. s i x
7. s e v e n   8. e i g h t
9. n i n e   10. t e n

Complete the block graph to show how many letters there are in each word.

number of words

4		ten		
3		six	nine	eight
2		two	five	seven
1		one	four	three
		3	4	5

number of letters

© HarperCollinsPublishers Spectrum Maths – Number: Teacher's Book 2

Main activity

▲ After the sheet has been completed, ask questions to help the children interpret the block graph, such as:
  • How many letters are there in the word 'three'? 'nine'...?
  • Which words have five letters? three letters...?
  • Which words have the same number of letters as the word 'seven'?
  • Which words have one letter fewer than the word 'four'?
  • Which word has as many letters as the number it spells?

Developments

▲ Extend the activity to include number words for the numbers eleven to twenty.

▲ Investigate, in the same way, number words from one to ten in other languages, e.g. in French:

no. of letters	2	3	4	5	6
	un	une	deux	trois	quatre
		six	sept		
		dix	huit		
			neuf		
			cinq		

Materials

▲ Number word cards (one–ten and eleven–twenty)

Individual practice in Workbook 2b
Activity 24 Names graph

Number words

Complete the number words.

1. o n e

2. t _ _ _

3. t _ _ _ _ _

4. _ _ _ _ _

5. _ _ _ _

6. _ _ _ _

7. _ _ _ _ _

8. _ _ _ _ _ _

9. _ _ _ _

10. _ _ _

Complete the block graph to show how many letters there are in each word.

number of words

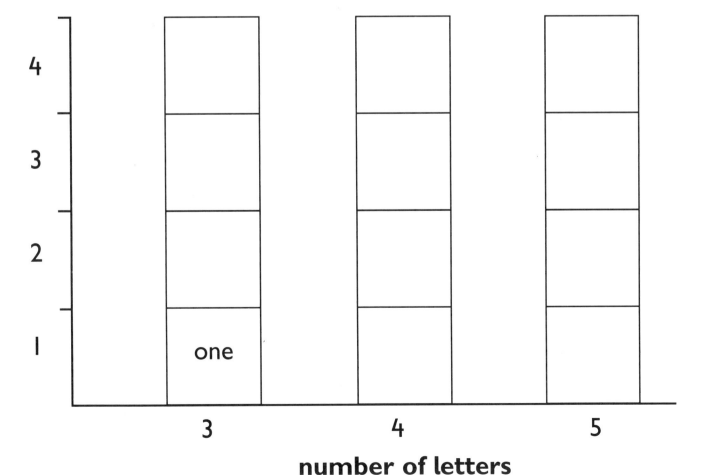

number of letters

Difference dog

Objectives

Understanding addition and subtraction
▲ Understand the operation of subtraction as 'difference'

Rapid recall of addition and subtraction facts
▲ Know subtraction facts for numbers to 10

Mental calculation strategies (subtraction)
▲ Find a difference by counting on from the smaller to the larger number

Reasoning about numbers
▲ Solve mathematical problems

Introducing the activity

▲ Clarify the concept of difference, using two towers of interlocking cubes of different heights. Explain that the difference is based on how many more are added to the smaller to make the larger tower.

▲ Extend this concept using a number line. Locate the two positions on the line and ask the children how many 'spaces' need to be jumped from the smaller number to reach the larger number. Emphasise 'spaces', not 'numbers'.

Main activity

▲ Before completing the sheet, remind the children that different pairs of numbers can have the same difference.

Developments

▲ Ask children to draw their own difference dog (or other creature) on squared paper, and then investigate the differences.

▲ Shuffle a pack of playing cards (take out the picture cards), and make two piles. Reveal the top card on each pile and ask the children to provide the difference between the two numbers. Continue through the pack.

▲ Extend the difference dog to contain numbers from 0 to 20, or 0 to 50.

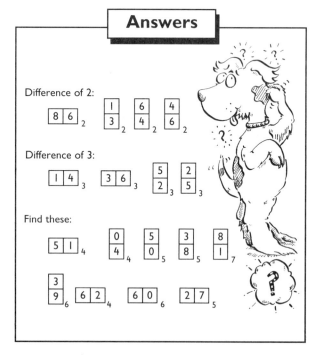

Answers

Difference of 2:

$\boxed{8\ 6}_2$ $\boxed{\frac{1}{3}}_2$, $\boxed{\frac{6}{4}}_2$, $\boxed{\frac{4}{6}}_2$

Difference of 3:

$\boxed{1\ 4}_3$ $\boxed{3\ 6}_3$ $\boxed{\frac{5}{2}}_3$, $\boxed{\frac{2}{5}}_3$

Find these:

$\boxed{5\ 1}_4$ $\boxed{\frac{0}{4}}_4$, $\boxed{\frac{5}{0}}_5$, $\boxed{\frac{3}{8}}_5$, $\boxed{\frac{8}{1}}_7$

$\boxed{\frac{3}{9}}_6$, $\boxed{6\ 2}_4$, $\boxed{6\ 0}_6$, $\boxed{2\ 7}_5$

Materials

▲ Interlocking cubes
▲ Number line (0–10)
▲ Squared paper
▲ Playing cards (without the picture cards)

Individual practice in Workbook 2b
Activity 25 Differences

Difference dog

□□₁ This means: Find the part of the dog which is this shape and has a **difference of one**. There are two.

Here is one. | 2 | 3 |₁

Can you find the other? □□₁

Find these difference pairs on the dog. They must all be different.

Difference of 2:

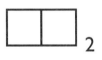₂ ₂ ₂ ₂

Difference of 3:

₃ ₃ 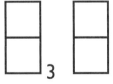₃ 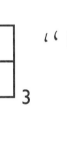₃

Find these:

₄ ₄ ₅ ₅ ₇

₆ 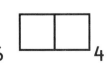₄ ₆ ₅

Back and front

Objectives

Understanding addition and subtraction

▲ Understand the operation of addition and recognise that it can be done in any order

▲ Begin to add three single-digit numbers mentally

Rapid recall of addition and subtraction facts

▲ Know addition facts for numbers to 10

Mental calculation strategies (addition)

▲ Add three small numbers by putting the largest first and/or find a pair totalling 10

▲ Add 9 by adding 10 and subtracting 1

Reasoning about numbers

▲ Solve mathematical problems

▲ Investigate general statements about numbers

▲ Explain methods and reasoning about numbers

Introducing the activity

▲ Practise adding three numbers, dealing number cards (1–10) out in sets of three. Discuss the fact that the order does not matter, and remind the children of the following strategies:
  - Start with the larger number
  - Look for pairs which add to 10
  - Add 9 by adding 10 then subtracting 1.

Answers

For the first set:

			total
2	1	3	6
2 1 6 or 5	1	3	9
2	8	3	13
2 8 6 or 5	8	3	16
5	1	6	12

For the second set:

			total
3	6	1	10
3	6	7	16
3	5	1	9
3	5	7	15
4	6	1	11
4	6	7	17
4	5	1	10
4	5	7	16

Main activity

▲ Ask the children: Which total is the smallest possible and which the largest?

▲ Discuss that in all cases there are 8 (2 × 2 × 2) different ways of arranging the three cards.

Developments

▲ Investigate how many of the possible totals are odd and how many are even.

▲ Ask the children to make their own set of three cards, with their own choice of six numbers, and to use them to investigate different possible totals.

Materials

▲ Number cards (1–10) (see photocopiable sheet on p.90)

▲ Square pieces of card

Individual practice in Workbook 2b
Activity 26 Totals
Activity 26b Rows and columns

Back and front

You will need:
three card squares

Write numbers on the front and back.

	front	back		front	back		front	back
1st card	2	5	2nd card	8	1	3rd card	3	6

Put the three cards in a line, like this, to show a total of 9.

1st	2nd	3rd	total
2	1	6	9

Arrange the three cards to show these totals.
Then write the numbers in the squares.

			total					total
☐	☐	☐	6		☐	☐	☐	16
☐	☐	☐	9		☐	☐	☐	12
☐	☐	☐	13					

Make three new cards like these.

	front	back		front	back		front	back
1st card	3	4	2nd card	6	5	3rd card	1	7

How many different totals can you make?

Make it smaller

You will need:
these number cards

Arrange them to make two 2-digit numbers that make this sentence true.

□□ is smaller than □□

<

Here are two ways.

1.

3 5 is smaller than 4 7

<

2.

4 3 is smaller than 7 5

<

How many other ways can you find?
Record your work here.

Subtracting with 6

Objectives

Understanding addition and subtraction
▲ Understand the operation of subtraction

Rapid recall of addition and subtraction facts
▲ Know subtraction facts for numbers to 10

Reasoning about numbers
▲ Solve mathematical problems, recognise simple patterns and relationships

Introducing the activity

▲ Practise subtraction using number cards (0–9). Draw a large outline of one of the incomplete subtractions on the sheet. Place number cards in position to create one possible correct subtraction. Check the accuracy of the subtractions by using either counters (take some away), or a number line (0–9) (count back along the line).

Answers

$6 - 1 = 5$	$7 - 6 = 1$
$6 - 0 = 6$	$8 - 6 = 2$
$6 - 2 = 4$	$9 - 6 = 3$
$6 - 3 = 3$	$7 - 1 = 6$
$6 - 4 = 2$	$8 - 2 = 6$
$6 - 5 = 1$	$9 - 3 = 6$
$6 - 6 = 0$	

Main activity

▲ Use number cards (0–9) and a subtraction outline for the children to experiment with different possibilities.
▲ Encourage the children to work systematically. For example, suggest they start by finding all the different subtractions which have 6 in the first box.

Developments

▲ Ask the children to find all the possible subtractions with at least one 4 in them. Extend this to other numbers. Is the total number of subtractions always the same?
▲ Extend to subtractions which involve subtracting a 1-digit number from a 2-digit number.
▲ Extend to finding all the additions with at least one 6 in them.

Materials

▲ Number cards (0–9) (see photocopiable sheet on p.90)
▲ Counters or a number line (0–9)

Individual practice in Workbook 2b
Activity 28 Taking away

Subtracting with 6

You will need:
number cards (0–9)

Use the cards to make different subtractions.
Each subtraction must have at least one 6 in it.

There are 13 altogether. Can you find them?
Write them down.
Two have been done for you.

6 − 1 = 5		6 − 0 = 6

$6 - 1 = 5$

$6 - 0 = 6$

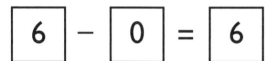
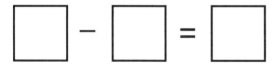
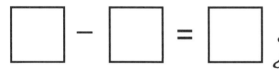
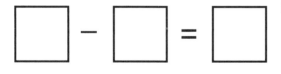
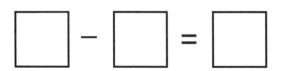
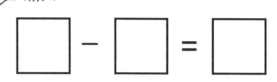
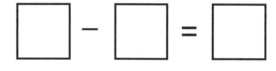

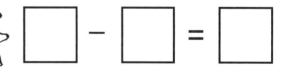

As near as you can

Objectives

Place value and ordering
▲ Read and write numbers to 100 in figures
▲ Know the value of each digit in a 2-digit number
▲ Understand and use the vocabulary of comparing and ordering 2-digit numbers
▲ Compare two 2-digit numbers, and say which is more or less

Estimating and rounding
▲ Round a 2-digit number to the nearest 10

Understanding addition and subtraction
▲ Understand the operation of subtraction as 'difference'

Mental calculation strategies (subtraction)
▲ Find a difference by counting on from the smaller to the larger number

Introducing the activity

▲ Using a 100 division number line, demonstrate the concept of 'nearness' of different 2-digit numbers to given targets. Choose a point on the line, then generate different 2-digit numbers using number cards (1–9), and see how close the numbers are to the chosen point.

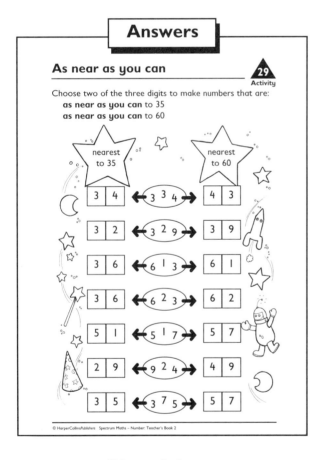

Main activity

▲ Discuss how many different 2-digit numbers can be made from one set of three digits (six can be made).
▲ Ask the children to explore how *far away* each of their numbers is from the target.

Developments

▲ Repeat the activity, using the same sets of digits, but changing the target, e.g. find the nearest to 25, to 50...
▲ Convert the activity into a game in which three dice are thrown to generate the three digits. Players arrange the digits to make 2-digit numbers close to given targets.
▲ Extend the activity to choosing two digits from four.

Materials

▲ Number line (1–100)
▲ Number cards (1–9)
(see photocopiable sheet on p.90)
▲ Dice

Individual practice in Workbook 2b
Activity 29 Nearest numbers

As near as you can

Choose two of the three digits to make numbers that are:
as near as you can to 35
as near as you can to 60

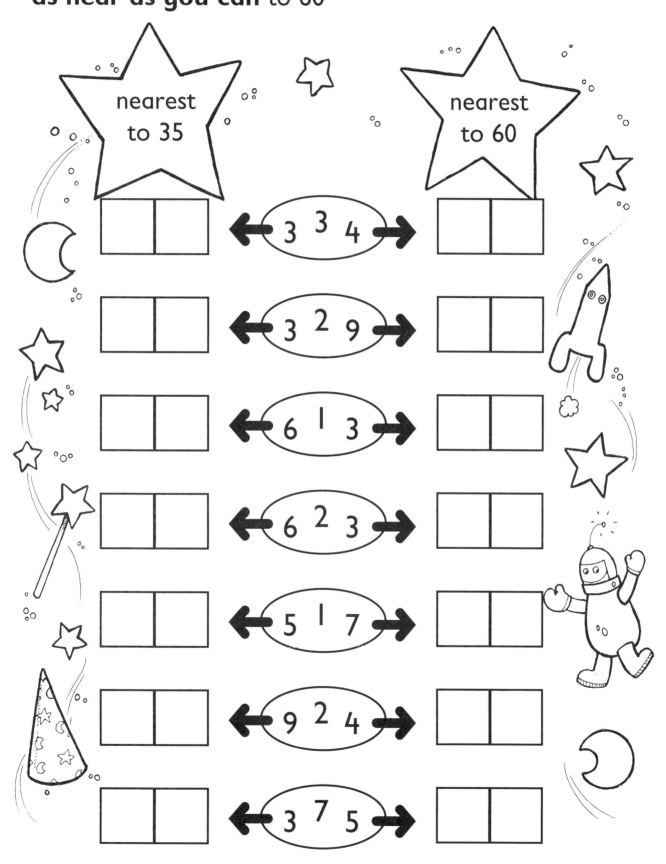

nearest to 35   3 3 4   nearest to 60

3 2 9

6 1 3

6 2 3

5 1 7

9 2 4

3 7 5

30 Activity

Lucky 13

Key vocabulary

dice
total

Objectives

Understanding addition and subtraction
▲ Understand the operation of addition, recognising that it can be done in any order
▲ Begin to add three single-digit numbers mentally

Rapid recall of addition and subtraction facts
▲ Know addition facts for numbers to 10

Mental calculation strategies (addition)
▲ Add three small numbers by putting the largest first and/or find a pair which totals 10
▲ Use patterns of similar calculations

Reasoning about numbers
▲ Solve mathematical problems, recognise simple patterns

Introducing the activity

▲ Practise finding the total of three dice. For example, play a game in which players take turns to throw the dice, and score points that match the total. Discuss strategies for adding the three numbers:
  • Start with the larger number first
  • Look for pairs which make 10.

Answers

There are five different ways of making a total of 13.
(6, 6, 1) (6, 5, 2) (6, 4, 3) (5, 5, 3) (5, 4, 4)

There are six different ways of making a total of 10.
(6, 3, 1) (6, 2, 2) (5, 4, 1) (5, 3, 2) (4, 4, 2) (4, 3, 3)

The number of different ways of finding other totals can be summarised in this table.

total	3	4	5	6	7	8	9	10
different ways	1	1	2	3	4	5	6	6
total	11	12	13	14	15	16	17	18
different ways	6	6	5	4	3	2	1	1

Main activity

▲ Some discussion may be useful to establish that:

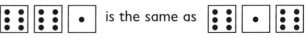

is the same as

▲ Encourage the children to work systematically. One strategy is to fix one dice, say at 6, and then try variations of the other two: (6, 6, 1), (6, 5, 2), (6, 4, 3) etc.

Developments

▲ Extend to numbering the dice differently, e.g. 3, 4, 5, 6, 7, 8.
▲ Extend to using four dice.

Materials

▲ Dice

Individual practice in Workbook 2b
Activity 30 Dice totals

Lucky 13

You will need:
three dice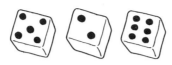

Here are two different ways
of throwing three dice
to make a **total of 13**.

    total 13   total 13

How many more ways can you find?
Record them here.

Find different ways to make a total of 10.

Coin tables

Key vocabulary

coin
row
column
total
amount
change

Objectives

Understanding addition and subtraction
▲ Understand the operation of addition, and use the related vocabulary
▲ Add more than two numbers (coins)

Rapid recall of addition and subtraction facts
▲ Know addition facts for numbers to 10

Mental calculation strategies (addition)
▲ Use known number facts to add mentally

Problems involving 'real life' or money
▲ Find money totals up to £1, and give change
▲ Recognise all coins and begin to use £.p notation

Introducing the activity

▲ Practise finding the total amount of sets of coins. Create five sets of coins, and label them a to e. Choose pairs of sets, e.g. c and d, a and d, and ask the children to provide the totals. Start with just one coin per set, then extend to more than one coin.

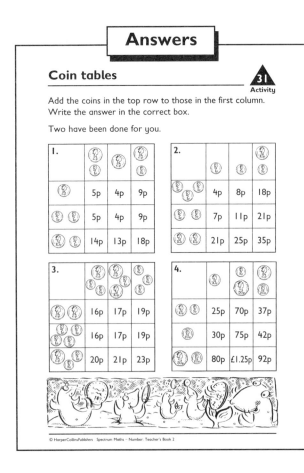

Main activity

▲ Show the children how to interpret the table, explaining that the entries represent the totals of the row and column headings.
▲ Discuss the terms 'row' (across) and 'column' (down).

Developments

▲ Look at each entry in the first grid in turn. Construct a new table which shows the amount of change from 50p for each answer. Extend this to change from £1.
▲ Children can create their own coin tables, using plastic coins placed on a large grid drawn on paper.
▲ Discuss different possible row and column headings which will give a given answer, e.g. 75p.

Materials

▲ Coins: 1p, 2p, 5p, 10p, 20p, 50p, £1

Individual practice in **Workbook 2b**
Activity 31 Adding money
Activity 31b Money totals

Coin tables

Add the coins in the top row to those in the first column.
Write the answer in the correct box.

Two have been done for you.

1.

	2p 1p	2p	2p 5p
2p	5p		
1p 1p			9p
10p 1p			

2.

		1p	5p	10p 5p
1p 1p 1p				
1p 5p				
10p 10p				

3.

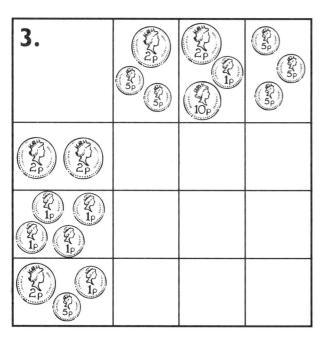

4.

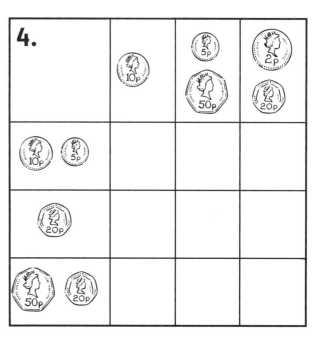

© HarperCollins*Publishers*   Spectrum Maths – Number: Teacher's Book 2

32

Activity

Matching game

Objectives

Rapid recall of addition and subtraction facts

▲ Know addition and subtraction facts for numbers to 10

Reasoning about numbers

▲ Solve mathematical puzzles

Introducing the activity

▲ Practise recall of the addition facts. Point at squares at random on the board. Ask the children to say the answer. Use a number line as a check, counting on from the larger number.

▲ Practise the subtraction facts, by using the number line and counting back.

Main activity

▲ Children play the game in pairs. Explain the rules:
  • The number cards (1–10) are dealt, ten to each player. Players can look at their cards.
  • Players take turns to play a card which matches the answer to one of the problems on the board, placing a counter on the appropriate square.
  • Counters cannot be placed on a square which already contains a counter.
  • The winner is the first player to make a straight line of four counters in any direction.
  • If all the cards are used before the end of the game, reshuffle, redeal and continue.

Developments

▲ Instead of dealing out the cards, place them in a pile, face down. Take turns to reveal the top card and attempt a match.

▲ Create an extended game, using cards with numbers greater than 10, and number facts to match the answers.

▲ Investigate different possible 'questions' for each answer. For example, how many of the squares on the board have an answer of 5? How many others could be created?

Materials

▲ Two sets of number cards (1–10) (see photocopiable sheet on p.90)

▲ Counters

> **Individual practice in Workbook 2b**
> Activity 32 Adding and subtracting

Matching game

You will need: two sets of number cards (1–10)
counters

5 − 3	2 + 2	4 + 6	3 + 6	1 + 2	6 − 1
5 + 1	9 − 5	3 − 2	5 − 2	10 − 3	7 + 3
4 + 4	7 − 5	1 + 7	3 + 2	9 − 7	7 − 5
6 − 5	4 + 1	8 − 2	5 + 5	3 + 4	7 + 2
2 + 6	6 − 2	10 − 8	6 + 1	10 − 9	2 + 4
1 + 3	5 + 3	3 + 3	10 − 5	4 + 5	2 + 5

Objectives

Understanding addition and subtraction
▲ Understand the operation of addition, recognising that it can be done in any order

Instant recall of addition and subtraction facts
▲ Know addition facts for numbers to 10

Mental calculation strategies (addition)
▲ Start with the largest number and count on in ones

Introducing the activity

▲ Practise adding two numbers, using a number line to help model the additions. Locate the first number on the line. Jump the appropriate number of 'spaces' along the line to match the second number. Emphasise 'spaces', not 'numbers'.

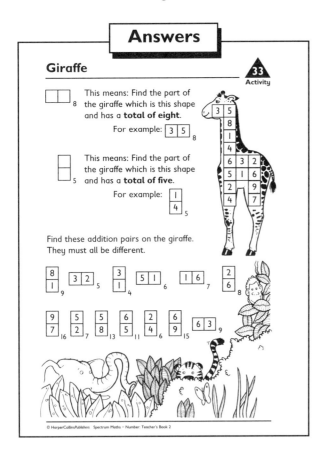

Main activity

▲ Before completing the sheet, explain that different parts of the giraffe might have the same total.

Developments

▲ Ask children to draw their own numbered giraffe (or other creature) on squared paper, and then investigate the totals.
▲ Extend the giraffe to contain numbers from 0 to 20, or 0 to 50.
▲ For further practice, shuffle a pack of playing cards (take out the picture cards), and make two piles. Reveal the top card on each pile and say the total of the numbers. Continue through the pack.

Materials

▲ Number line (1–20)
▲ Squared paper
▲ Playing cards or number cards (1–10)
(see photocopiable sheet on p.90)

Individual practice in Workbook 2b
Activity 33 Find the numbers

Giraffe

This means: Find the part of the giraffe which is this shape and has a **total of eight**.

For example:

3	5
$_8$

This means: Find the part of the giraffe which is this shape and has a **total of five**.

For example:

1
4
$_5$

Find these addition pairs on the giraffe. They must all be different.

$_9$ $_5$ $_4$ $_6$ $_7$ $_8$

$_{16}$ $_7$ $_{13}$ $_{11}$ $_6$ $_{15}$ $_9$

Left or right?

Activity 34

Key vocabulary

left/right
grid
row/column

Objectives

Data handling

▲ Extract and interpret data presented in Carroll diagrams

Introducing the activity

▲ Clarify the construction and interpretation of a Carroll diagram:
  • Draw the outline of a 2 × 2 grid on the board, and also draw a larger 2 × 2 grid to represent the diagram on the floor.
  • Make labels on card of your chosen four headings, e.g. boys, girls, straight hair, curly hair. Put them in the appropriate place around the Carroll diagram on the floor.
  • Choose a number of children from the class and sort them into two groups according to one criterion, e.g. *boys v girls*. Arrange them in two rows.
  • Choose another criterion, e.g. *straight hair v curly hair*. Arrange the children on the Carroll diagram on the floor.
  • Transfer the card headings to the diagram on the board and record the children's names, under the correct headings.

▲ Ask questions about the diagram you have created (see Main activity below for ideas).

Answers

	boys	girls
left-handed	Stanley	Karen Shireen
right-handed	Jake Gurdeep Peter	Jenny Emma Honor Tracy

Main activity

▲ After the sheet has been completed, ask questions to help children interpret the diagram:
  • How many left-handed boys/right-handed girls are there?
  • Is Jenny, Jake... left- or right-handed?
  • Which girls are left-handed? Which boys are right-handed?
  • Which girls are not right-handed?
  • How many girls are included altogether? How many boys?
  • How many children altogether?
  • How many altogether are left-handed? How many right-handed?
  • Which group has two children? Which has three?
  • How many more are right-handed than left-handed?

Developments

▲ Collect data for children in the class based on the same two criteria, and draw the matching Carroll diagram.

▲ Draw Carroll diagrams based on different criteria, such as:
  • Hair: *curly v straight* and *short v long*
  • Beetroot: *boys v girls* and *likes beetroot v dislikes beetroot*.

Materials

▲ Four large sheets of paper
▲ Card

Individual practice in Workbook 2b
Activity 34 Sorting

Left or right?

Write the names on the diagram.

Fives and tens

Objectives

Counting and properties of numbers

▲ Count on or back in steps of 5
▲ Recognise multiples of 2, 5 or 10

Reasoning about numbers

▲ Recognise and predict simple number patterns

Introducing the activity

▲ Using a large 100 square, highlight the sequences covered on the sheet. For example, practise counting in fives from 5 to 100 and point at the numbers on the square as you do. Do this again, but without looking at the square. Repeat, but count backwards instead of forwards.
▲ Extend to counting in twos and tens.

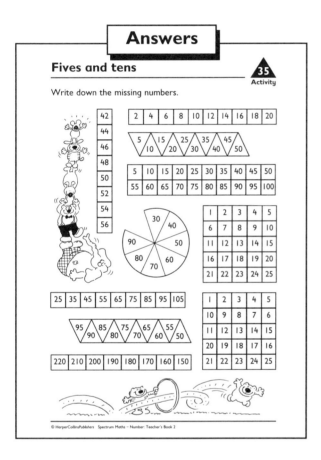

Main activity

▲ When the sheet is completed, ask the children to colour squares to highlight patterns, e.g. colour squares which contain a multiple of 10 in the same colour. Colour the remaining multiples of 5 (5, 15, 25...) in another colour.

Developments

▲ Investigate how many times particular numbers appear on the sheet.
▲ Children create their own sequences on squared paper, e.g. sequences which jump in 25s or 50s.

Materials

▲ Squared paper

Individual practice in Workbook 2b
Activity 35 Twos, fives and tens

Fives and tens

Write down the missing numbers.

42
44
46

2	4	6	8					

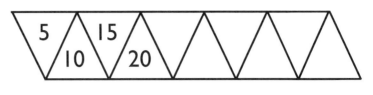

5 / 10 15 / 20 ...

5	10	15	20	25					50
55	60			80			95		

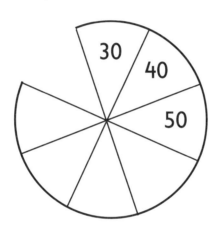

30 40 50

1	2	3	4	
6	7	8	9	10
11				

25	35	45						

95 / 90 85 / 80 ...

1	2	3	4
		8	7	6
11	12			
	19			16

220	210	200	190				

36 Activity

Odd dice

Objectives

Counting and properties of numbers
▲ Recognise odd and even numbers

Reasoning about numbers
▲ Solve mathematical problems

Introducing the activity

▲ Clarify the distinction between odd and even numbers. Throw one dice and discuss whether the throw is even or odd. Throw pairs of dice and ask the children to say whether they show 'both odd', 'both even' or 'one odd and one even'. Extend this to throwing three dice.

Answers

There are ten different 'all odd' combinations.

1	1	1		1	5	5
1	1	3		3	3	3
1	1	5		3	3	5
1	3	3		3	5	5
1	3	5		5	5	5

Main activity

▲ Start by discussing 'different' arrangements. Discuss, for example, that (1, 3, 5) is the same set of dice as (3, 5, 1), but in a different order.
▲ Discuss methods of recording, i.e. draw the dots on squares, or write the numbers.
▲ Encourage a systematic approach, e.g. start with one dice showing 1, and investigate what the other two dice might show.

Developments

▲ Investigate the different possible totals of three-dice throws.
▲ Ask questions such as: If one dice shows 3, one shows 1 and the total is 9, what does the third dice show?
▲ Ask the children to investigate the possibilities of making a total of 10 with two odd dice and one even dice. In how many different ways can this be done? Extend to other totals.
▲ Extend the activity to showing even numbers only.
▲ Extend to showing one odd and two even numbers.
▲ Investigate the possible ways of showing only odd/even numbers using three spinners numbered 1 to 10.

Materials

▲ Dice
▲ Spinners (1–10)

> **Individual practice in Workbook 2b**
> Activity 36 Odds, evens and totals

Odd dice

You will need:
three dice

Here are two ways to arrange the dice to show
odd numbers only.

   1   3   3   5   1   1

How many different ways can you find altogether?
Record your work here.

Difference pyramids

Objectives

Understanding addition and subtraction
▲ Understand the operation of subtraction as 'difference'

Rapid recall of addition and subtraction facts
▲ Know subtraction facts for numbers to 10

Mental calculation strategies (subtraction)
▲ Find a difference by counting on from the smaller to the larger number

Reasoning about numbers
▲ Explain methods and reasoning about numbers

Introducing the activity

▲ Clarify the concept of difference, using two towers of interlocking cubes of different heights, e.g. of height 3 and 5. Explain that the difference is based on how many more need to be added to the smaller to make the larger tower.

▲ Extend this concept using a number line. Locate the two positions on the line and ask the children how many 'spaces' need to be jumped from the smaller number to reach the larger number. Emphasise 'spaces', not 'numbers'.

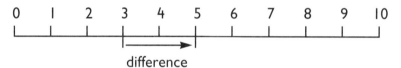

difference

Main activity

▲ Complete the sheet. Notice that in these examples, the top numbers are all 0, 1 or 2. Is this always the case? Ask the children to investigate.

Developments

▲ Construct a difference pyramid which has a given top number, e.g. 5. Write 5 on the top brick, then write two numbers below it which have a difference of 5, e.g. 1 and 6, and so on.
▲ Construct pyramids of different sizes.
▲ Instead of building the pyramids based on differences, base them on totals. For example, if two adjacent bricks contain 2 and 6, then the brick directly above contains 8.

Materials

▲ Pyramid paper (see photocopiable sheet on p.93)

Answers

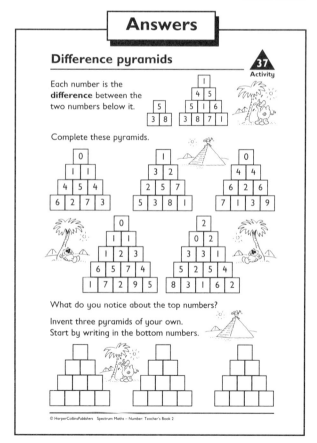

Individual practice in Workbook 2b
Activity 37 More differences

Difference pyramids

Each number is the **difference** between the two numbers below it.

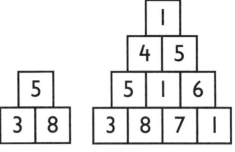

Complete these pyramids.

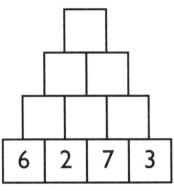

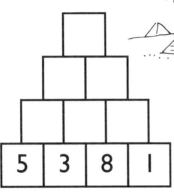

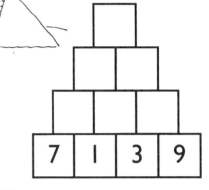

| 6 | 2 | 7 | 3 |

| 5 | 3 | 8 | 1 |

| 7 | 1 | 3 | 9 |

| 1 | 7 | 2 | 9 | 5 |

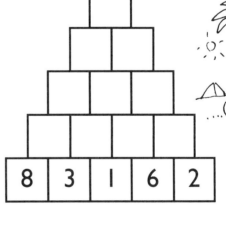

| 8 | 3 | 1 | 6 | 2 |

What do you notice about the top numbers?

Invent three pyramids of your own.
Start by writing in the bottom numbers.

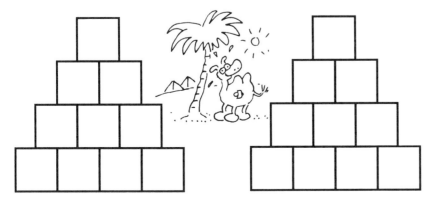

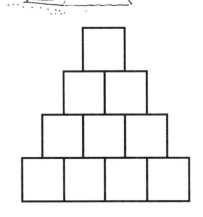

Fill them up

Objectives

Estimating and rounding

▲ Begin to read and use the vocabulary of estimation

Problems involving measures

▲ Use the vocabulary related to capacity, estimate and measure capacity using non-standard units (e.g. yoghurt cartons)

Data handling

▲ Collect, represent and interpret numerical data in simple tables

Introducing the activity

▲ Discuss the term 'capacity' (how much a container will hold). Ask the children to compare, by eye, two containers and to estimate which has the larger capacity. Test their answer by pouring from one container to the other.

▲ Measure the capacity of each container by using a non-standard unit, e.g. a tin. Ask the children to estimate how many 'tin-fuls' each container will hold. Measure by filling and pouring repeatedly from the tin.

Main activity

▲ The children should play the game in pairs. Explain the rules:

• Start by choosing one of the containers.
• Each player guesses how many yoghurt cartons full of water will fill the container.
• Record the guesses on the score sheet.
• Next, measure to find out how many pots of water are needed.
• The player whose guess is the closest to the actual measure wins the round.
• Repeat for the other containers.
• The overall winner is the player who wins the most rounds.

container	guess		number of cartons	winner
	A	B		
bowl	6	10	9	B
jar				

Developments

▲ Use a different non-standard measure, e.g. a cup.

▲ Players score points equal to the difference between their guess and the actual measure. The winner is the player with the lowest total difference.

Materials

▲ A set of containers (jar, bowl, bottle, jug, pot...)
▲ Yoghurt cartons of the same size
▲ Water

Individual practice in Workbook 2b
Activity 38 Full or empty?

Fill them up

You will need:

a set of containers
yoghurt cartons

container	guess		number of cartons	winner
	A	**B**		

container	guess		number of cartons	winner
	A	**B**		

More machines

Key vocabulary

times
multiply
divide
times-table

Objectives

Understanding multiplication and division
▲ Understand the operations of multiplication and division

Rapid recall of multiplication and division facts
▲ Know the multiplication facts for the 2 and 10 times-tables and begin to know the 5 times-table
▲ Derive quickly the division facts corresponding to the 2 and 10 times-tables

Introducing the activity

▲ Rehearse counting in twos, tens and fives.
▲ Introduce the concept of multiplication by collecting sets of two objects, then ten and then five.
▲ Use sets of feet to develop the 2 times-table with the class: 'One child has two feet, two children have four feet, three children have six feet...'. Record this at each stage as 1 × 2 = 2, 2 × 2 = 4, 3 × 2 = 6..., saying 'one two is two, two twos are four, three twos are six...'. Consolidate by asking questions like: 'How many feet do six children have?' Use the children to count in twos.
▲ Consolidate the concept of division by asking questions like: 'If there are ten feet, how many children are there?'
▲ Ask children to hold out both hands to show ten fingers and develop the 10 times-table. Then hold out one hand to show five fingers for the 5 times-table.

Answers

The completed tables are:

×2		×10		×5		÷2		÷10	
in	out	in	out	in	out	in	out	in	out
3	6	2	20	3	15	10	5	30	3
5	10	3	30	5	25	8	4	80	8
2	4	4	40	10	50	14	7	100	10
7	14	7	70	2	10	20	10	60	6
4	8	8	80	6	30	2	1	50	5
1	2	9	90	1	5	8	4	90	9
10	20	1	10	4	20	12	6	40	4
8	16	6	60	7	35	16	8	70	7

Main activity

▲ Discuss the multiplication and division machines and the different operations for these tables.
▲ Children can use feet and fingers to help consolidate the facts, or, alternatively, use towers of five interlocking cubes to illustrate the multiplication/division facts for 5, for example.

Developments

▲ Introduce different machines, e.g. a doubling machine, a halving machine (see Activity 17).
▲ Use addition machines (e.g. 'Add 5') or subtraction machines (e.g. 'Take 3'), ensuring that numbers fed into the 'Take 3' machine are all 3 or more.
▲ For further practice, make sets of double-sided cards, each side a different colour. On one side, write the numbers from 1 to 10. On the reverse side, write the product of multiplying that number by 5 – for example, 7 on the front and 35 on the back. The children use these to practise learning the multiplication and division facts for the 5 times-table.

Individual practice in Workbook 2b
Activity 39 Twos, tens and fives

More machines

This is a × 2 machine.

When 3 is put **in** the machine, **out** comes 6.

Complete this table for the × 2 machine.

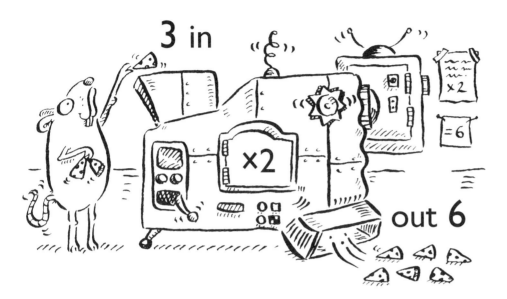

in	out
3	6
5	
2	
7	
4	
1	
10	
8	

Complete the tables for these machines.

in	out		in	out		in	out		in	out
2			3			10			30	
3			5			8			80	
	40		10			14			100	
	70		2			20				6
8			6			2			50	
	90		1			8				9
1			4			12			40	
6			7			16			70	

Near things

Key vocabulary

digit
2-digit
number
nearest
difference

Objectives

Place value and ordering

▲ Understand and use the vocabulary of comparing and ordering 2-digit numbers
▲ Compare two 2-digit numbers, and say which is more or less

Estimating and rounding

▲ Round a 2-digit number to the nearest 10

Understanding addition and subtraction

▲ Understand the operation of subtraction as 'difference'

Mental calculation strategies (subtraction)

▲ Find a difference by counting on from the smaller to the larger number

Introducing the activity

▲ Use a 10 division number line, and label it 0 to 100 instead. Give the children practice in locating the positions of various numbers on the line.
▲ Choose a position on the line, e.g. 30. Choose two other numbers, e.g. 21 and 43, and discuss which is the closer to 30. Illustrate by using the line to find how far each number is from 30. Repeat this activity for different examples.

Answers

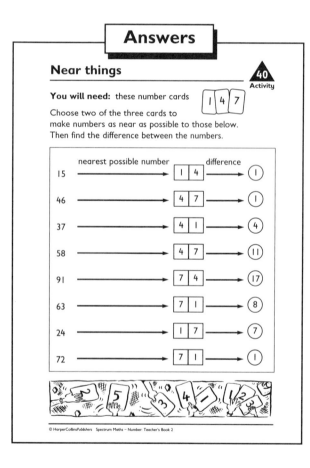

Main activity

▲ Discuss how many different 2-digit numbers can be made with the cards 1, 4 and 7. (Six are possible: 14, 17, 41, 47, 71, 74.)
▲ After completing the nearest numbers, ask the children to find out how far away each number is from its target (i.e. find the difference between the two numbers).

Developments

▲ Investigate the nearest possible number to 10, 20, 30... to 100.
▲ Try the same activity, but with a different set of three cards.
▲ Repeat the activity, this time choosing from four cards.
▲ Extend to 3-digit numbers.
▲ Instead of making numbers near to others, make them as far away as possible.

Materials

▲ Number line (0–100)
▲ Number cards (1–9)

Individual practice in **Workbook 2b**
Activity 40 Target numbers
Activity 40b Nearest

Near things

You will need: these number cards

Choose two of the three cards to
make numbers as near as possible to those below.
Then find the difference between the numbers.

	nearest possible number	difference	
15	⟶	1 4 ⟶	◯
46	⟶	4 7 ⟶	◯
37	⟶	⬜ ⟶	◯
58	⟶	⬜ ⟶	◯
91	⟶	⬜ ⟶	◯
63	⟶	⬜ ⟶	◯
24	⟶	⬜ ⟶	◯
72	⟶	⬜ ⟶	◯

Number cards

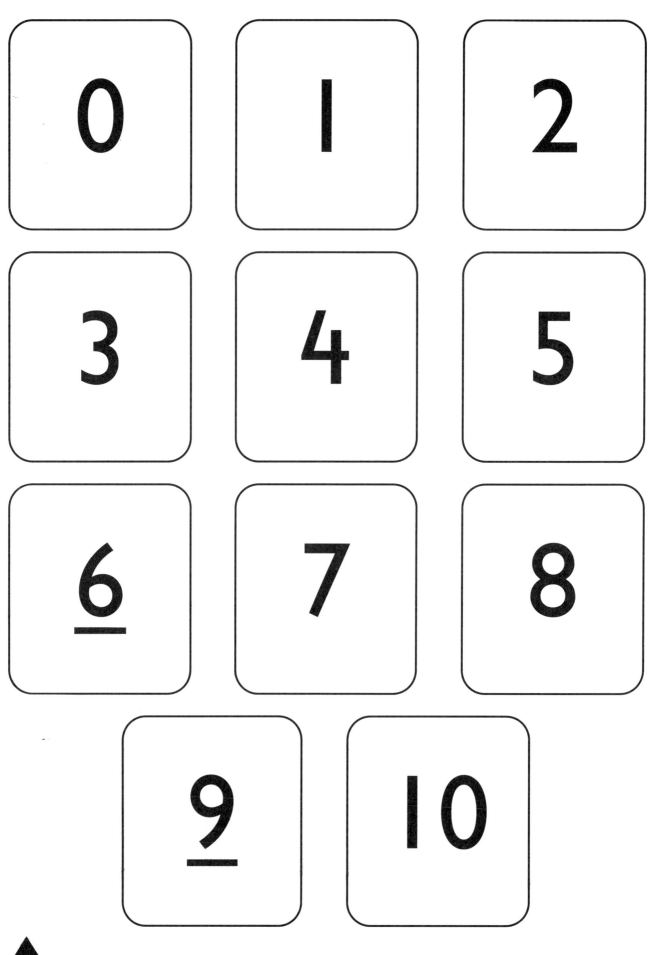

0 1 2 3 4 5 6 7 8 9 10

See-saw paper

Block graph paper

Title:

8

7

6

5

4

3

2

1

Pyramid paper

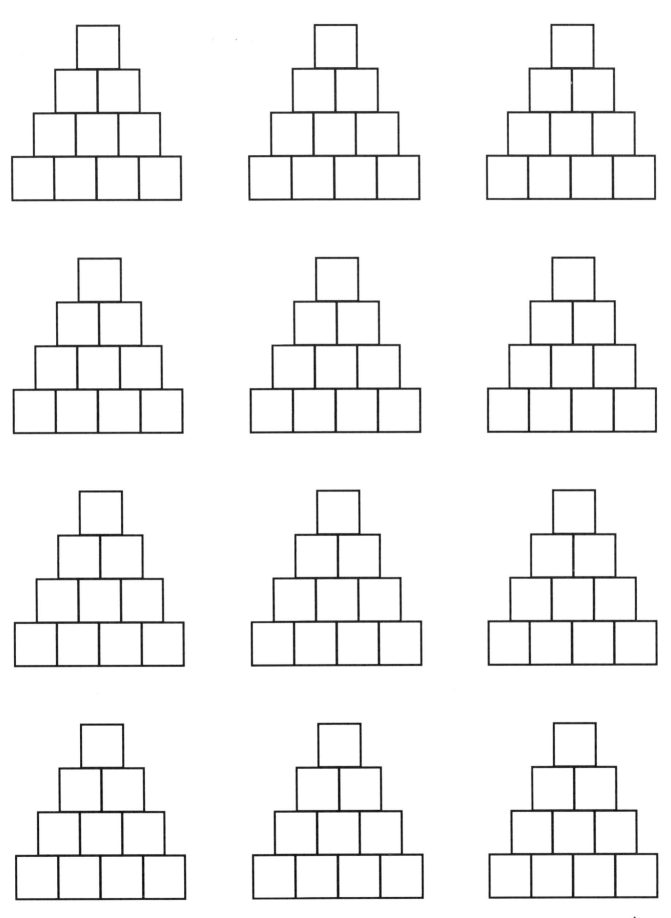

Workbook answers

Workbook 2a

Activity 1 Adding up
1. 3 + 5 = 8   2. 2 + 4 = 6
3. 4 + 2 = 6   4. 5 + 1 = 6
5. 6 + 3 = 9   6. 3 + 2 = 5
7. 5 + 2 = 7   8. 6 + 4 =10
9. 2 + 2 = 4   10. 3 + 3 = 6
11. 4 + 4 = 8   12. 5 + 5 = 10
13. 8 + 1 = 9   14. 6 + 5 = 11
15. 1 + 6 = 7   16. 2 + 9 = 11
17. 10 + 3 = 13   18. 5 + 10 = 15

Activity 2
Totals and differences

	total	difference
1.	8	2
2.	6	2
3.	5	1
4.	8	0
5.	7	3
6.	7	5
7.	9	3

Activity 2b
More totals and differences

	total	difference
1.	10	4
2.	7	3
3.	10	2
4.	8	6
5.	10	6
6.	13	5
7.	7	1
8.	8	4

Activity 3 Missing numbers

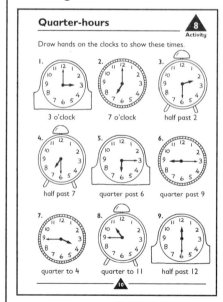

Activity 4
Telephone numbers
1. 7   2. 2   3. 1
4. 4   5. 8   6. 6
7. 9   8. 3   9. 5
10. 3   11. 7

Activity 5
Largest and smallest
1. 75   2. 86   3. 54
4. 96   5. 87   6. 74

in order: 54, 74, 75, 86, 87, 96

7. 13   8. 14   9. 35
10. 24   11. 17   12. 34

in order: 35, 34, 24, 17, 14, 13

Activity 6 Height
From left to right, the heights of
the flowers are:
3 cm, 4 cm, 8 cm,
7 cm, 9 cm, 5 cm

Activity 7
Balance the numbers
1. 4   2. 7   3. 2
4. 5   5. 13   6. 6
7. 6   8. 4   9. 10
10. 7   11. 6   12. 5
13. 8   14. 2   15. 8

Activity 8 Quarter-hours

Activity 9 Taking away
Check the children have coloured
the hexagons correctly.
blue (answer 1)
10 − 9, 6 − 5, 8 − 7, 4 − 3
green (answer 2)
8 − 6, 10 − 8, 9 − 7, 7 − 5
yellow (answer 3)
9 − 6, 7 − 4, 6 − 3, 10 − 7, 8 − 5
red (answer 4)
9 − 5, 7 − 3, 8 − 4, 6 − 2, 10 − 6

Activity 9b
More taking away
1. 7 − 5 = 2   2. 9 − 1 = 8
3. 10 − 4 = 6   4. 9 − 4 = 5
5. 8 − 6 = 2   6. 9 − 7 = 2
7. 8 − 1 = 7   8. 5 − 3 = 2
9. 3 − 2 = 1   10. 10 − 3 = 7
11. 7 − 3 = 4   12. 10 − 5 = 5
13. 10 − 8 = 2   14. 7 − 5 = 2
15. 6 − 2 = 4   16. 10 − 1 = 9

Activity 10
Adding three numbers
1. 2 + 1 + 3 = 6
2. 4 + 3 + 2 = 9
3. 3 + 2 + 5 = 10
4. 6 + 1 + 2 = 9
5. 4 + 4 + 1 = 9
6. 1 + 2 + 7 = 10
7. 4 + 2 + 3 = 9
8. 5 + 3 + 2 = 10
9. 1 + 2 + 3 = 6
10. 2 + 5 + 1 = 8
11. 3 + 3 + 2 = 8
12. 3 + 5 + 4 = 12

Activity 11 Block graph

fruit	votes
banana	5
apple	2
grapes	3
pear	4

Activity 12 Coin totals
1. 8p   2. 14p   3. 16p
4. 6p   5. 9p   6. 21p
7. 23p   8. 31p   9. 17p
10. 27p

Activity 13
Find the difference
1. d = 2   2. d = 2   3. d = 4
4. d = 4   5. d = 1   6. d = 5
7. d = 3   8. d = 1   9. d = 5
10. d = 5   11. d = 2   12. d = 2
13. d = 7   14. d = 7   15. d = 7

Activity 14 Ordering
1. 17   19   23   29   35   42
2. 25   26   29   30   31   33
3. 25   28   29   36   39   47
4. 17   18   19   20   21   22
5. 52   50   49   47   36   25
6. 46   38   31   27   25   19
7. 95   86   81   72   62   43
8. 74   60   49   35   29   26

Activity 15 Number pairs
The complete pairs are:
1. 10, 10   5, 15   19, 1   16, 4
2. 20, 10   15, 15   5, 25   28, 2
3. 20, 30   40, 10   25, 25   5, 45
4. 50, 50   40, 60   30, 70   90, 10
5. 3, 5 or 1   8 or 4, 6
   4, 6 or 2   9 or 5, 7
6. 2, 7   8, 3   1, 6   9, 4
7. 3, 13   15, 5
   12, 22 or 2   24 or 4, 14

Activity 16 Tens and units
1. 5   2. 20   3. 70
4. 8   5. 5   6. 20
7. 30 + 6   8. 40 + 8
9. 70 + 2   10. 80 + 5
11. 40 + 9   12. 60 + 8
13. 64   14. 73   15. 19
16. 27   17. 35   18. 91

Activity 17
Doubling and halving
1. 6, 12, 10, 16, 8, 18
2. 8, 5, 2, 10, 7, 3
3. 20, 80, 10, 40, 100, 60

Activity 18 Clues
Check the children have coloured
in the following numbers:
1. 9 to 13 inclusive
2. 27, 29, 31, 33, 35
3. 52, 54, 56, 58, 60
4. 33 to 41 inclusive
5. 76, 78, 80, 82, 84, 86

Activity 19 Fractions
1. $\frac{1}{2}$ 2. $\frac{1}{4}$ 3. $\frac{1}{4}$ 4. $\frac{1}{2}$

5. $\frac{1}{2}$ 6. $\frac{1}{2}$ 7. $\frac{1}{2}$ 8. $\frac{1}{4}$

9. $\frac{1}{2}$ 10. $\frac{1}{4}$

Activity 20 Pairs
1. 11   2. 10   3. 9   4. 15
5. 13   6. 11   7. 4   8. 6
9. 2   10. 5   11. 4   12. 8
13. 10   14. 40   15. 50

Activity 20b Pairs to 20
Check the children have joined
the correct pairs.
14 + 6, 12 + 8, 17 + 3, 11 + 9,
19 + 1, 16 + 4, 13 + 7, 15 + 5,
2 + 18

Workbook 2b

Activity 21 Centimetres
a. 7 cm   b. 3 cm   c. 5 cm
d. 12 cm   e. 10 cm   f. 4 cm
g. 13 cm   h. 6 cm   i. 8 cm

Activity 22
Large, small, odd, even
1. 71, 74, 17, 14
2. 65, 62, 25, 26
3. 83, 84, 43, 34
4. 31, 32, 13, 12
5. 85, 84, 45, 48
6. 67, 76, 27, 26

Activity 23 What's next?
1. 8, 10, 12, 14
2. 7, 9, 11, 13
3. 22, 20, 18, 16
4. 25, 23, 21, 19
5. 12, 15, 18, 21
6. 20, 25, 30, 35
7. 16, 20, 24, 28

Activity 24 Names graph

number of letters	frequency
3	4
4	4
5	3
6	2
7	2

Activity 25 Differences

Activity 26 Totals
1. 6   2. 8   3. 11   4. 9
5. 8   6. 12   7. 10   8. 14
9. 5   10. 3   11. 4   12. 5

Activity 26b
Rows and columns
1. column totals: 8, 13, 11
   row totals: 12, 10, 10
2. column totals: 9, 11, 10
   row totals: 12, 6, 12
3. column totals: 15, 18, 12
   row totals: 17, 13, 15
4. column totals: 14, 21, 10
   row totals: 11, 14, 20

Activity 27 Smaller or larger
1. 43 < 58   2. 47 < 62
3. 83 > 19   4. 45 > 44
5. 27 < 35   6. 48 < 63
7. 75 > 71   8. 19 < 20
9. 20 < 29   10. 41 > 38

For questions 11 to 16, check the
children have written in
appropriate digits.

Activity 28 Taking away
1. 5   2. 5   3. 4   4. 2
5. 6   6. 7   7. 1   8. 1
9. 5   10. 3

5, 1, 3, 6, 4
3, 6, 1, 5, 2

Activity 29 Nearest numbers

The following numbers should be coloured in:

1. 20	2. 30	3. 30
4. 20	5. 20	6. 30
7. 40	8. 40	9. 50
10. 70	11. 30	12. 10
13. 60	14. 50	15. 60
16. 80	17. 90	18. 40

Activity 30 Dice totals

1. 7	2. 9	3. 10	4. 11
5. 12	6. 16	7. 11	8. 13
9. 15	10. 10		

Activity 31 Adding money

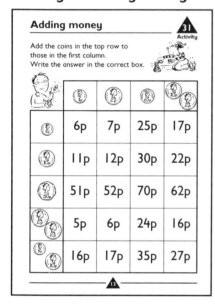

Activity 31b Money totals

1. 9p	2. 18p	3. 37p
4. 35p	5. 28p	6. 65p
7. 57p	8. 45p	

Activity 32
Adding and subtracting

Check the children have coloured the boxes correctly, and written additions and subtractions with an answer of 10.

yellow (answer 6) 8 − 2, 1 + 5, 3 + 3, 2 + 4, 7 − 1, 9 − 3, 6 + 0, 10 − 4

green (answer 7) 10 − 3, 3 + 4, 8 − 1, 9 − 2, 6 + 1, 5 + 2

blue (answer 8) 4 + 4, 3 + 5, 9 − 1, 10 − 2, 2 + 6

red (answer 9) 2 + 7, 10 − 1, 8 + 1, 4 + 5, 6 + 3

Activity 33 Find the numbers

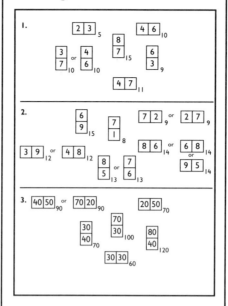

Activity 34 Sorting

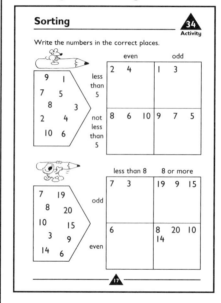

Activity 35
Twos, fives and tens

The complete sequences are:

1. 10, 15, 20, 25, 30, 35, 40, 45
2. 10, 20, 30, 40, 50, 60, 70, 80
3. 42, 40, 38, 36, 34, 32, 30, 28
4. 100, 95, 90, 85, 80, 75, 70, 65
5. 110, 120, 130, 140, 150, 160, 170, 180
6. 4, 6, 8, 10, 12, 14, 16, 18
7. 5, 15, 25, 35, 45, 55, 65, 75
8. 10, 30, 50, 70, 90, 110, 130, 150

Actvitiy 36
Odds, evens and totals

Check the children have coloured the odd dice yellow and the even dice blue.

1. 5	2. 9	3. 7
4. 6	5. 8	6. 11
7. 6 even	8. 9 odd	
9. 11 odd	10. 15 odd	

Activity 37 More differences

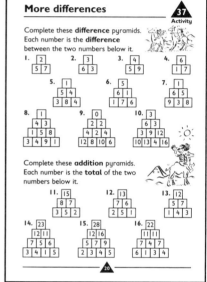

Activity 38 Full or empty?

1. half full	5. full
2. nearly empty	6. nearly full
3. nearly full	7. empty
4. full	8. half full

Activity 39
Twos, tens and fives

1. 10	2. 8	3. 14
4. 12	5. 16	6. 20
7. 3	8. 9	9. 1
10. 2	11. 70	12. 40
13. 30	14. 60	15. 5
16. 9	17. 15	18. 30
19. 40	20. 45	21. 2
22. 5		

Activity 40 Target numbers

1. 73	2. 52	3. 64	4. 13
5. 57	6. 49	7. 61	8. 46
9. 73	10. 38		

Actvity 40b Nearest

1. 46	2. 15	3. 39
4. 48	5. 55	